Irene S. Moore, C.S.

THE HIGHER ORDER OF SCIENCE

Identity

by

IRENE S. MOORE, C.S.
Author of *The Bridge*

DeVorss & Co.—Santa Monica, California

Copyright © 1974 by Irene S. Moore

ISBN: 0-87516-192-8

Library of Congress Catalogue Card No. 74-81338

Printed in the United States of America by
DeVorss & Co., 1641 Lincoln Blvd., Santa Monica, Calif. 90404

ABOUT THE AUTHOR

Born in New York City, Mrs. Moore was educated in local schools. Her first Christian Science membership was in *Eighth Church,* New York City, where she was a member of various committees. Subsequently moving to Connecticut, she transferred her membership to the Greenwich *Church of Christ, Scientist.* While there she served as Assistant Librarian, Sunday School teacher, Church Treasurer, and member of the Executive Board. She had class instruction with an authorized teacher in 1950 and became listed in *The Christian Science Journal* as a practitioner in 1955. Soon after this Mrs. Moore moved to California and transferred her church membership to *Twenty-Eighth Church* in Los Angeles. She served on several committees here also. She was Chairman of the Lecture Committee prior to writing her book, *The Bridge.* Because of its publication she was excommunicated from both the Christian Science church organization and her branch church in 1972.

I lovingly dedicate this book to the individuals who had the courage to attend my classes on *The Higher Order of Science.*

May I repeat what I read in class from *Prose Works*:

> You are the needed and the inevitable sponsors for the twentieth century, reaching deep down into the universal and rising above theorems into the transcendental, the infinite—yea, to the reality of God, man, nature, the universe . . . . You go forth . . . with loving look and with the religion and philosophy of labor, duty, liberty, and love, . . . Your highest inspiration is found nearest the divine Principle and nearest the scientific expression of Truth.[1]

---

1. *My.* 248:13-18, 26-30.

ABBREVIATIONS

used in the footnotes for the writings of Mary Baker Eddy
in their final revised form (as of 1910).

Mis.	Miscellaneous Writings
My.	The First Church of Christ Scientist and Miscellany
No.	No and Yes
Pul.	Pulpit and Press
Ret.	Retrospection and Introspection
S. & H.	Science and Health with Key to the Scriptures
Un.	Unity of Good

References to *The Holy Bible* are found in the *Authorized King James Version*, printed by *Oxford University Press*.

PREFACE

I am Soul's substance, the Word and the power,
Life, Truth and Love, the might and the tower,
The light and the glory of all that began.
How great is this Allness, this Allness, man.
All of the joy, the fullness, the might
Is being the beauty, the kingdom, the light!
I feel Love's sublimity, know God's Allness as "Day,"
The Christ full appearing, "Now and Alway."[1]

This book is a record of the talks given at the 1973 classes held in Los Angeles, California. Its purpose is to inspire the student to identify with the higher order of Science. This concept of Science is, in truth, the higher order of One's Self; it is found to be our very own God-conscious identity. In other words, we are the essence of spirituality in our physical form, and we joyously accept this today: the divine oneness of our Being, the glory of the God-Being which we are.

Since writing *The Bridge* I have received many letters from those who have read the book and frequently they wrote of their identification with the ideas in it. Some said they felt they had written it themselves because their own experiences related so clearly to what I had written. Therefore, with permission of the writers, I am sharing with you several of their letters.

---

1. Irene S. Moore, C.S.: *The Bridge,* p. 236, Poem: *Identity.*

I have taken the definition of God to be found in the *Glossary* of *Science and Health with Key to the Scriptures* by Mary Baker Eddy, and have accepted it as the basis of our work in identifying as the I Am. I feel that the synonyms for God which we studied in this class are the very source and foundation of our being. Identifying as Principle, Mind, Soul, Spirit, Life, Truth, Love, substance and intelligence permits us to have a spiritual awareness of our progressive life and its divinity here and now. In these classes we discussed the method of translation as a way of maintaining the wholeness and Oneness which constitute our higher order of Science. We continue to give our wholehearted attention to our Christliness, thereby expressing the full stature of Man as our Present Being.

Irene S. Moore, C.S.
Los Angeles, California

IDENTITY

Today, as students who are consciously aware of a
higher order of Science, we are being very modern by
the attention we give to the subject of *Identity*. It is
of common interest in the world, coming to our attention from numerous walks of life. Many young people are eager to identify with the central character of
what has come to be known as the Jesus movement;
older persons are reminding us of their rights as experienced individuals; women are asking for a greater
share of life's fullness. We can understand these things
clearly if we do not have preconceived and judgmen-
tal attitudes about them, and if we make positive and
loving efforts to comprehend the reasons for their happenings.

Women are moving seriously into politics, into medi-
cine and engineering. They are asking for the same
civil rights men have. It is the issue in the 27th
Amendment to the Constitution of the United States,
presently in process of ratification by the various members of the Union. Black Americans are identifying
with what they call a "black culture." They, too, seek
equality of opportunity and an identification with all
that the "white culture" stands for. Many mature people are identifying as Senior Citizens, certainly a more
dignified recognition than that which merely saw them
as older persons. Nor is orthodox religion standing still.
We are all aware of the great reforms appearing in

1

the Roman Catholic Church. Among other things many priests no longer wish to be celibate; they seek the right of marriage if they choose it.

Evangelism is making great strides persuading people to make "commitments to Christ." Think of the many meetings held by Billy Graham, by Oral Roberts and by Kathryn Kuhlman, with her special type of gospel healing. They are demonstrating the universal power of Christianity. Many other more orthodox religious leaders give recognition to these spiritual healings, seeing them as coming from the one divine Source even though they, themselves, do not preach an evangelistic religion. All these changes come about by individuals breaking away from traditional ideas and by their making an identification with new ones at the same time.

James R. Adair, in his book, *We Found Our Way Out*,[1] describes his interviews with serious and dedicated persons who had felt themselves captive to the beliefs of certain religious or social groups to which they belonged but who were finally able to free themselves. The book explains very well why they left their organizations: they were seeking something that was not to be found there, namely, an understanding of their personal/spiritual identities.

In a book titled *Future Shock,* by Alvin Toffler, it is brought out that new identities arise when changes in our experience take place. The author predicts that these changes will be coming to us at an increasing rate. How one responds to these changes and how he will accept the new identities that appear are some of

1. James Adair and Ted Miller: *We Found Our Way Out.* Baker Book House, Grand Rapids, Mich., 1964.

the questions that he discusses in his book. He tells us:

> . . . We don't want to hear things that may upset our carefully worked out structure of beliefs . . . [They threaten] to undermine our carefully worked out style of life . . . But when our style is suddenly challenged, when something forces us to reconsider it, we are driven to make another super-decision. We face the painful need to transform not only ourselves but our self-image as well.[2]

In other words, we are moving beyond the old order. Our reconsiderations have developed a new order, a new identity, sometimes out of the old—and may I add here, incidentally, that it need not be a painful adjustment just because it is described this way. Again he says:

> . . . We become in some sense, a different person, and we perceive ourselves as different. Our old friends, those who knew us in some previous incarnation, raise their eyebrows. They have a harder and harder time recognizing us, and, in fact, we experience increasing difficulty in identifying with, or even sympathizing with, our own past selves . . . [The new order] presents the individual with a contest that requires self-mastery and high intelligence.[2]

This book will give you marvelous insight into many of the changes which are taking place today and why

2. Alvin Toffler: *Future Shock*. Random House, Inc., New York, 1970, pp. 278, 279, 282, 283.

they are occurring. Toffler does not always offer solutions to the enormous questions that are arising in our society but he does bring in much to consider, not just the personal changes we make in ourselves or the developing cultural attitudes of young people, but even such matters as the effects on mankind of the growing bureaucracy of our times! I was particularly interested in a chapter titled, *Organization: The Coming Adhocracy,* in which organizational entity is described as gradually collapsing for the reason that man is not the dependent person he used to be. Today man is feeling the power of his own spiritually individual growth, and his expansion on this is inevitable.

You and I are being called to identify with a higher order of Christian Science. The first thing to do about this is to recognize ourselves in a new dimension—one that *actualizes* us as *Mind*—one that sees each personal activity as *Mind manifest.* We, too, are leaving the old for the new, sometimes almost imperceptibly, sometimes abruptly, but however it may be described we move inevitably to new ways of consciousness and, therefore, of living. We, too, are experiencing wonderful revolutionary changes within us; we are not standing still. We receptively consent to this new identity in which we are actualized as Mind. It is a progression beyond orthodox Christian Science concepts, from which we look back to see how beautiful our unfoldment has been. Our God-consciousness is ever with us; our gratitude for it continues to be found in all the steps along the way.

Updating our Science, as we are doing today, is, in fact, giving it a practical and spiritual place in our

lives. I know that each person who is in this class will
walk out in the same physical form he had when he
walked in, but when he leaves he surely will have an
extended consciousness of his identity as Mind, as Principle, as Soul, as Spirit, Life, Truth, and Love. He also
accepts the statement from Psalm 46:10, "Be still, and
know that I *am* God: . . ." as referring to himself,
*knowing that he is the I AM and that God is his spirit-
ual consciousness.*

Many consecrated students of Christian Science are
now identifying this way and it is quite different from
their identification in the past. Some have written
books which describe their progressive unfoldment into
the recognition of a new identity in themselves. Several
of them I have mentioned in chapters of *The Bridge,*[3]
but there are many others which you can find in the
reference list in the back of that book.

One day I was sent a copy of the magazine *New
Thought,* Winter, 1972 in which there was a review of
The Bridge. Looking through it I saw an advertisement
of a book by Dr. Cushing Smith, C.S.B., titled, *I Can
Heal Myself And I Will.*[4] This sounded a little like "Be
still, and know that I am God . . ." so I ordered it and
subsequently read it interestedly. Dr. Smith was courageously presenting *his* Science of Being *as he understood it* without concern for criticism or reproof, ad-
vocating that students treat themselves through denial
of error and affirmation of Truth, a rather orthodox
approach, of course, but in this case with variations on

3. Irene S. Moore, C.S.: *The Bridge,* DeVorss and Co., Santa Monica,
Calif. 1971, pp. 378, 379, 380.
4. Cushing Smith, CSB, Ms.D.: *I Can Heal Myself and I Will,* Frederick
Fell, Inc., New York, 1962.

the usual theme. One of the chapters is called *Meta-physician, Heal Thyself*. I wrote to him expressing my appreciation for the effort he put into his work, and I informed him about the book I had written on Christian Science, of course from a very different premise. He ordered it and soon I received this letter:

> . . . first, let me tell you how deeply your own book, *The Bridge,* is appreciated by all in my household. It certainly bridges the gap between what Mrs. Eddy intended and what she has been mistakenly accused of saying.
>
> Your book is written for the experienced Scientist, while mine is intended for 'the man in the street' in line with what M.B.E. wrote: 'The remedy consists in probing the trouble to the bottom, in casting out by *denial* the error of belief which produces a mortal disorder . . .' But, as you so definitely point out, *there is nothing working but the ONE MIND.*
>
> I still feel that the study of what Jesus did and declared in the four Gospels is my main interest. His were the teaching which Mrs. Eddy illuminates in her writings. However, to understand Jesus as she reveals him is a necessary step in the unfoldment, and *your book is essential to understanding what she wrote.*
>
> Most Appreciatively,
Dr. Smith.

I never cease to be grateful for the inspiration which is mine as I go on with my work in the higher order of (Christian) Science. It involves much, but more than anything it strengthens my understanding of who I am and how I exist as Mind's consciousness.

―――――――

The meaning I take for the word "identity" is *the acceptance of my divine nature,* the acknowledgment of the divinity of my personal life *in the flesh* incorporating me as a spiritual idea at the same time. So I think I should begin my class with a discussion of the higher order of Identity that exists as each of us.

I want to emphasize this word, this idea, because through my correspondence and the meetings I have had with Christian Scientists since I wrote *The Bridge,* I have been surprised to find that although students have spent many years in the organization doing the Lesson-Sermons, attending lectures and listening to Association Addresses, many of them hesitate to identify themselves as ". . . [a] spiritual identity in the likeness of the divine; . . ."[5] or as the ". . . identity, or idea, of all reality [that] continues forever; . . ."[6] Both of these quotations are from *Science and Health.*

In traditional Christian Science one does not accept Man as his present spiritual identity, and I mean Man as we acknowledge him in the flesh with all his senses. I feel certain that the chapters in *The Bridge* titled *Man, Present Being* and *Person* have underlined the importance of this more refined understanding. In the higher order of Identity our objective is precisely this: "Fixing your gaze on the realities supernal, you will

―――――――

5. *S. & H.* 51:8
6. *S. & H.* 71:5

rise to the spiritual consciousness of being, even as the bird which has burst from the egg and preens its wings for a skyward flight."[7] Incidentally, the marginal heading for this quotation is "Immutable identity of man." Let us note: Mrs. Eddy says *you* will rise, not someone else, and *you do it at the time you are occupied with supernal realities!* She is writing to you as a person; you are reading what she has written as a person, and she recognizes the potential *in your person.* And "Fixing your gaze on the realities supernal . . . ," may I add, is exactly what we are doing in our work today by recognizing ourselves as the identity of Spirit, here, presently, in the flesh. What we have to do to make our accomplishment a present one is to delete the word "will" from the statement quoted above. Then we come naturally into the realization that the "rise to spiritual consciousness" is happening to us right now. This brings to us the point of realization.

I was not surprised to find Webster's dictionary defining the word "identity" as "sameness of essential character . . . oneness . . . unity . . ," and in this connection let us this moment remember a statement which underlines this thought: "Spirit is not separate from God. Spirit *is* God."[8] Let us boldly identify ourselves as this Spirit, this God-Being which is to each his very own self!

———

The *Glossary* provides us with the first definition of God: *I AM.* We recognize at once our Oneness-rela-

7. *S. & H.* 261:27-30
8. *S. & H.* 192:9-10

tionship to this I AM as our own God-consciousness. Accepting this, we see the higher order of all things *as our personal identity*. Of course, there are many reasons why some students of Christian Science do not dare to identify as I am describing it. Their religious concepts get in the way of their Scientific ones even though in Truth they are each a facet of the One Consciousness concept.

The higher order of the Bible is a source of great substance. (You know the Bible has its higher order, too!). You may recall my explanation in *The Bridge* of the developing God concept in the Bible as it appeared to several persons in these scriptures:

> Moses, who could not look at the face of God and live,
> David, who was going to awake in God's likeness,
> Jacob, who saw the face of God in Esau, and
> Jesus, who stated "I and my Father are ONE."

The higher order of your Divinity identifies itself spiritually as you recognize that you are living the I AM in physical form and substance as your God-likeness. Rejoice in this actuality! When we use the word "substance" we mean the something we see as we look out upon our universe with a vision of perfection. Our perception is the reality of our God-experience, the feeling of it made concrete as our present-day living. Part of our universe this moment is sitting here in this room, and at noon-time it will be such a natural activity as having our lunch. Not only see but *feel* all activities as your present reality, your conscious awareness of living your I AM.

In the definition for God in the *Glossary,* the phrase "I AM" is capitalized, as are all the synonyms. The capitalization is meant to imply that these words are reserved for Deity. Using capitals, however, is merely a holdover from traditional religion that sees Deity and the synonyms separate from ourselves. Read *Miscellany* on *Capitalization,* pages 225-226. You may remember the gratitude I expressed to a friend who brought out how often we use the term "I AM" in the ordinary conversations we have about our daily activities. We use this phrase all the time. In its true spiritual sense we are referring to ourselves. The "I AM" is not something belonging to Deity apart from what we are. It is a very important expression of our own divinity, our all-knowing, all-seeing, all-acting, all-wise, all-loving and eternal God-Being, our completely full and potential awareness of Divinity.

Remember these words of Jesus: "I am the way, the truth, and the life . . ,"[9] ". . . I am not come to destroy, but to fulfil,"[10] and ". . . I am come that they might have life, and that they might have *it* more abundantly."[11] The same I AM which we find in the definition of God, and which we so easily associate and identify with Jesus, is the I AM as Us. *The application of this*—the acknowledgment that we are this I AM— *is the fulfillment of our own identity.*

We read in *Misc. Writings* "Christ was 'the way;' since Life and Truth were the way that gave us, through a human person, a spiritual revelation of

---

9. *John* 14:6
10. *Matthew* 5:17
11. *John* 10:10

man's possible earthly development."[12] Yes, and Life and Truth continue this revelation through ourselves. It is not something that was merely for Jesus to experience. His identity he defined in his statement: ". . . he that hath seen me hath seen the Father; . . ."[13] It must be our statement as well in order to give us the opportunity to do the ". . . greater works . . ." Identify in the way Jesus did for your own fulfillment of I AM.

Each of us has his unique spiritual function within the context of his own I AM. Your acknowledgment of this fact today, in this class, may be the most important thing that is happening to you. Our own individuality directs and leads us in specialized ways according to the infinitely wonderful spiritual/material differences that distinguish our personalities. No two of us are alike in this grand diversity of expression. It is most important for you to know that there is something for *you* to do with *your* special higher order of Identity— something that only you, humanly, can do—something set aside for your talents, your spiritual qualifications. It does not need to be a complicated activity; some of the simplest works are most effective, some of the plainest most beautiful.

In orthodox Christian Science we were so busy getting rid of that which did not belong to us that we were apt to overlook what we spiritually/materially are. Many times we were identifying as important what did *not* belong to us more than what was in truth our Christ-consciousness. In the higher order of Identity, however, your own Science of Being is seen and felt

---

12. *Mis.* 75:2-5
13. *John* 14:9

as concrete, visible, form activity, and the joy of all this
is that it not only appears tangible as yourself but you
recognize it everywhere else, and I mean in all aspects
of your life—*all of them.* Oh, the relief in not working to annihilate human concepts or to unsee the ma-
teriality of the universe! What a joy it is to see it all
as our present divinity!

One time when I was serving on a Flower Committee at church several members brought flowers
from their gardens, and those experienced in flower-
arranging showed the others what could be done with
the flowers and the containers we had on hand for
such purpose. On my way home after the meeting, I
stopped at the grocery store a few blocks from the
church. While I was there I met a friend who was also
returning from the meeting. She looked at me and
said, "From the sublime to the ridiculous!" Of course
I knew exactly what she meant. She was reminding
me how sublime had been the atmosphere at the meeting with the Flower Committee and, by comparison,
how "ridiculous" was our presence in the grocery store.
It seemed to her that she had suddenly plunged into a
situation that was a disparaging one—even a mockery
when she compared it to the committee meeting. I
knew this member fairly well so I took her by the hand
and brought her to the counter where the fruit and
vegetables were on display. I pointed out that all the
lovely colors we had seen at our flower-arranging committee meeting were also here, merely in another form,
beautiful to behold. The divinity of the flowers, their
form and fragrance, had been moved in us to another
manifestation of the infinite variety of Mind, this time
in a different character: the fragrance of strawberries,

of oranges and lemons, and the colors of lettuce, cucumbers and radishes. I felt she understood what I was saying. In leaving the church we were not leaving our divinity behind; we took it with us and now we were seeing it manifest in another place! We were simply wandering through our world of beauty in the grocery store just as we had at the Flower Committee meeting.

The higher order of Identity secures us to a spiritual consciousness of loveliness everywhere. It deletes ideas of separation so that the continuity of our divine Being is something we can experience all the time and in every place. In other words, we now live the life divine in all areas of existence. We don't just read about it and anticipate its appearance sometime in the future.

Oh yes, I know all the thoughts that would argue with this higher identity. One, for example, is this: "The corporeal senses can take no cognizance of spiritual reality and immortality."[14] Well, my friend may have accepted this as Truth, and with such an understanding she would naturally believe she viewed her grocery store items with senses that she wished she could be without! In that case, of course, she would not have been able to appreciate their true beauty, for to her it would not be beauty! But *now that we have crossed our bridge our sense of matter is different. It has been lifted up.* Mrs. Eddy said, "Christ Jesus' sense of matter was the opposite of that which mortals entertain . . ."[15] True, she is seeing differences in Jesus' sense of matter compared to that of "mortals," but at least

14. *S. & H.* 488:20-21
15. *Mis.* 74:13-14

she saw that there is a higher degree of matter after all and Christ Jesus exemplified it. He said for us to ". . . Go, and do . . . likewise." (Luke 10:37). Does not this mean that we also have this higher order of Matter to put to work in our lives? *The Bridge* states this in many different ways. Most assuredly, the work on "I AM" that we are doing right now follows directly from our understanding of the higher order of matter as well as that of identity. It gives us a higher order of God.

Here is a letter I would like to share with you to show you how this person's concept of matter was developing. The quotation is in a letter from a friend of hers who had shared *The Bridge* with someone she knew.

> What a wonderful present arrived for me this morning — of course, it was the wonderful book. It certainly promises to be good. I have read the Introduction and can only say that it is all my own experience. How I am looking forward to feasting on it. You know, we have been 'growing' this book and its crystal clear view for a very long time. We have passed from one writer to another but always on a higher level of awareness, with Oneness as our main point. From what little I have read, Mrs. Moore brings out clearly the Oneness. Do you remember when we used to go through the Scientific Statement of Being but always leaving out the denial aspect 'Matter is mortal error, etc.' and this shows how our divinity even then, was unfolding itself as our

humanity. Now we are seeing and knowing that these are not two, but One. *All* is our infinite Self, as Manifestation.

As part of the same letter my friend writes, "Just thought you would be interested in her comments."

In *The Los Angeles Times* a movie called *The Ruling Class* was advertised. I have not seen the picture so I do not know of its content, but I *do* know that I read a wonderful conversation in the advertisement. Someone is asking one of the characters "How do you you know you're God?" And his answer is: "Simple. When I pray to Him I find I'm talking to myself." Isn't this enlightening! An appeal to God is *an appeal to the higher order of One's Self!* Shakespeare says: "Our remedies oft in ourselves do lie, which we ascribe to Heaven."

Many years ago a beautiful poem was sent to me. It is revolutionary in its meaning and presentation. When I first read it I still had a God concept far removed from the nearness I understand today as omnipresence. But this poem challenged my thought. It gave me another dimension of God more meaningful to the increasing awareness of my universe and it emphasized the *I* of my Being. The new view came to me in such a way that I understood God to be as close to me as my own breath! Here is the poem.[16]

---

16. Author unknown

MASTERY

I at last have reached the Goal
And solved the mystery of my Soul.
I am that to which I prayed,
To which I looked for aid.
I am that which I did seek;
I am my own mountain peak;
I upon creation look
As a leaf in my own book.
For I, The One, "the many" make
Of substance which from me I take.
For all is me, there are no two;
Creation is myself all through.
What I grant unto myself
I take down from my own shelf
And give to me . . . The Only One . . .
For I am the Father and the Son.
When I want I do but see
My wishes coming forth in me;
For I am the knower and the known,
Ruler, Subject and the Throne.
The "Three in One" is what I am.
Hell itself is but a dam
Which I did put in my own stream
When in a nightmare I did dream . . .
That I was not that Only One.
Thus by me was pain begun,
Which ran its course till I awoke
And found that I with me did joke . . .
So now that I do stand awake,
I my throne do wisely take
And rule my Kingdom, which is me:
A Master through Eternity.

It is interesting to note that the author of the poem is unknown, and I almost believe this was intended so that each reader may happily identify himself as the ". . . Master through Eternity." After all, Paul tells us to ". . . come boldly unto the *throne of grace* . . ."[17] In the higher order of Identity we are there.

————

Traditional Christian Science is presented in such a way that it often separates us from I AM because we are taught that only God is I AM. We are shown in many ways that it is not ourselves in our physical form — maybe after the "transition," ("Probation After Death") but not now by any means. *Yet, now is the time to accept this high estimate of ourselves* in every situation and to know that "The Scriptures [have declared] *Life* to be the infinite I AM, . . ."[18] They are referring to *your* life and *your* I AM. And we gratefully go right on accepting that this gives man ". . . not merely a sense of existence, but an accompanying consciousness of spiritual power . . ."[19] If you look up these citations in your books do not be surprised to find that I have deliberately deleted the remainder of the sentences. I do it purposefully because there are contradictions in the statements if you continue. However, we are grateful for the references that are almost complete in themselves, such as the one found in *My.* 132: 16 through 21, ending with the word "divine." Cannot one be healed of the thought that only God is I AM?

17. *Hebrews* 4:16 (Italics mine)
18. *Mis.* 189:20-21
19. *Mis.* 189:22-24

Cannot this identification with I AM be your experience today? I say it is yours right now, has always been and is eternally established.

In *S. & H.* 253:7-8 we find this: "I am the substance of all, because I AM THAT I AM." Isn't this glorious! Claim it for yourself today! Accept it as the present abundance of your divine Being! All substance, yours, as I AM. You know so well what it means to have the power of the Word within you that you find yourself expressing gratitude for all things *before* receiving them.

One of the testimonies I heard at a Wednesday evening service was from the soloist. She stated that she had tried to get a substitute to sing for her that evening because her home was in great danger of being burned in a fire and she felt her place was with her family. In her testimony she expressed gratitude for the wonderful sense of peace and assurance she had about this situation, but the most inspiring thing about it was that she closed the testimony with these words: "Father, I thank thee that thou hast heard me. And I [know] that thou hearest me always . . ."[20] She was giving thanks before she had any evidence of her home being untouched by the fire. This is a higher order of Gratitude. We later learned her home had remained free from any damage whatsoever.

See yourself joyously giving thanks for everything *before* the evidence of what you so prayerfully desire to identify as your life. Don't just say the words. Feel and acknowledge them. Remember that "Divine Love always has met and *always* will meet every human

20. *John* 11:41-42

need."[21] Understanding this to be true, you need never be concerned about anything. This is just another way of knowing your identity to be divine Love. Love is your identity and your divinity *now*. Love meeting your every need is the divine Love that is what and where you are. That is why it is met. It is not outside your consciousness.

Do you remember the poem "Substance" in *The Bridge* on pages 44 and 45? That poem was written soon after someone called me for an understanding of a higher order of Supply. We recognize substance as evidence of God-conscious Self relative to infinite supply. It is essentially knowing that:

> All substance, Soul, as my own Being,
> Unfolds as that which I am seeing.

As we identify Substance within our consciousness it is more than seeking and asking for something—it is confidently and assuredly *knowing* this fullness and completeness within us, the presence of infinite substance. ". . . all that I have *is* thine."[22] Emphasize the *is* in this acceptance. Realize that you have all that you need now. Your God-consciousness includes all, and understands substance as "I AM ALL . . ." In the reference that states Man ". . . represents infinite Mind, the sum of all substance"[23] and in the marginal heading on the same page titled "God's man discerned," recognize your self as that Man. *Identify.* In the very moment of reading that "All substance, in-

---

21. *S. & H.* 494:10-11 (Italics mine)
22. *Luke* 15:31 (Italics mine).
23. *S. & H.* 259:4-5

telligence, wisdom, being, immortality, cause, and effect belong to God"[24] take a giant step and *know* that these things are yours. The moment you read that "The universe . . . expresses the divine substance or Mind; . . ."[25] it is *your Mind* that is presently being expressed. When you open your concordances, select from them all the wonderful statements regarding substance as it is viewed from this high order. Then, in each reference, let yourself say *"That's me! That's what I AM!"* All that is I AM as substance is yours eternally and forever. Your substance is ". . . self-existent and eternal Mind; that which is never unconscious nor limited."[26] Accept this as your spiritual heritage. ". . . the kingdom of God [all substance, Spirit] is within you."[27] This is your fulfilled supply.

When a friend sent me a copy of *The Edinburgh Lectures on Mental Science* my higher order of Identity reminded me that I was my own authority and that I had the right to read it if I wished. Having marked a few passages, I thought I would share some of them with you because they bring out the same idea that fulfillment of all our desires comes through beautifully with proper expectation and realization:

> An ideal, as such, cannot be formed in the future. It must either be formed here and now or not be formed at all and it is for this

24. *S. & H.* 275:14-15
25. *S. & H.* 300:28-29
26. *S. & H.* 588:24-25
27. *Luke* 17:21

reason that every teacher, who has ever spoken with due knowledge of the subject, has impressed upon his followers the necessity of picturing to themselves the fulfillment of their desires as *already accomplished* on the spiritual plane [this plane], as the indispensable condition of fulfillment in the visible and concrete.

When this is properly understood, any anxious thought as to the *means* to be employed in the accomplishment of our purposes is seen to be quite unnecessary . . . we have to work upon them, not with fear, doubt, or feverish excitement, but calmly and joyously, because we *know* that the end is already secured . . .

If his wishes are in line with the forward movement of the everlasting principle there is nowhere in Nature any power to restrict him in their fulfillment.[28]

One of the important reasons for my writing *The Bridge* was to take away all guilt and condemnation from students, to introduce them to a clear and practical realization of their individual divinity in every situation and to have them fully appreciate their personal higher order of Identity. This understanding lifts up the "I" of their Christ-consciousness and, whatever the circumstances, keeps it lifted up. In the chapter, *Man, Present Being* in *The Bridge,* I described what

28. Thomas Troward: *The Edinburgh Lectures on Mental Science,* Dodd, Mead & Company, New York, 1909, pp. 59, 67, 68, (Italics mine).

I called my Divinity Course. Identity played a very great part in it.

From a book entitled, *Life and Teaching of the Masters of the Far East,* by Baird T. Spalding, I quote:

> . . . the moment a man accepts himself as less than the King, less than his Divinity, he has thereby become less than his own Kingship. It is far better to say, 'I can' and then go right on to 'I AM.' 'I can' is the potential fact, but 'I AM' is its fulfillment in your consciousness.
>
> Even your ability to analyze the 'I AM' is a direct spiritual evidence of Divinity.[29]

This book came to me from my niece. I was delighted to find in it many thoughts which supported my premise of *Oneness.* Much of it is a statement of my own spiritual unfoldment out of orthodoxy. When Truth is stated clearly, in the presence of a receptive consciousness, we readily identify with it. May I add here that there is no need to be reluctant to read any metaphysical book. Inspiration is universal and comes from many sources. We know we are selective in our reading and we can choose what we wish to accept. Now here is another important thought from the book I have just mentioned:

> It is not what man studies, but how he studies that is the secret of illumination.[29]

Starting with the knowledge that he *is* Truth, Life

29. Baird T. Spalding: *Life and Teaching of The Masters of The Far East,* Volume IV. DeVorss & Co., Santa Monica, California, 1948, pp. 106, 117, 121, 118.

and Love, as well as all the other synonyms for God, one receives more from his studies than if he were to approach them with a feeling of lack and that the book is going to supply that lack. One day I visited a patient in her home. She had beside her stacks of *Sentinels* and *Journals* which she had been eagerly going through. When I asked her what she was looking for, she said she was looking for a testimony in the periodicals from someone who had been healed of an ailment like hers, and she had not found such a testimony. I looked at her and said, "Well then! I guess there is no healing for you!" She was startled by my statement but recovered her composure when I told her she *could* begin with the premise that she was whole, perfect and harmonious *now* and that she could admit her own healing first without necessarily looking for accounts of others' healings. After this she began working very differently in Christian Science. I had taken an opportunity to introduce her to a higher order of her identity, a God-conscious, present awareness of her own divinity. Not only was she healed of the difficulty but with her understanding she found added joy. Since then she has often pointed out to me wonderful statements of Truth, Life and Love she was now making her own with her liberated view of Science. Every student receives something from his efforts in his study of Christian Science but *knowing* first of all *one's spiritual identity* presents a more ready realization of one's perfection of Being.

Imagine my surprise when I came to this in the Spalding book, page 97, (italics mine) :

We cannot stop in our progress with organizations and systems either orthodox or metaphysical, for they are sectional, sectarian, and teach a doctrine that is more or less involved with the idea of separations. *They are only steps in the process of man's discovery of himself.* We cannot stop at any point without becoming orthodox. That prevents further progress until we break away.

That is where so many people become mixed in affirmations and denials . . . They fasten to themselves a condition that does not exist, and then when they feel this false influence of their own mental reaction they call it malicious-animal-magnetism.

I must assume from this last statement that the author knew something about orthodox Christian Science and the dualistic premise upon which it is founded.

―――――――

Now let us accept this following statement as relating to ourselves, Spirit. "Spirit is the only substance and consciousness recognized by divine Science."[30] Isn't this truly wonderful as you identify consciously as it? You see, you are recognizing the higher order of Christian Science which is divine Science. As divine Science you recognize your divinity, Spirit. Today you know that you are not only the Science of Being but through the study of *The Bridge* you have come to know you are divine Science, and you understand why.

―――――――

30. *S. & H.* 278:4-5

It is because you have accepted your higher order of Identity as Spirit now. And ". . . the divine Science which ushered Jesus into human presence, will be understood and demonstrated"[31] by *you,* and *you* go right along happily identifying with 1st. Cor. 13:12, ". . . then shall I know even as also I am known."

With all the statements of Truth we have been considering and with which we have so beautifully identified, this next one is the full and complete statement of what we are as I AM: "This supreme potential Principle reigns in the realm of the real, and is 'God with us,' the I AM."[32] Divine Science, our realm of conscious reality, is expressed as "God with us," and if God is with us, all the attributes of God are us as "I AM." Principle which reigns as us is the reality of our own Being, the present law and order of our glorious personal/spiritual identity. This consciousness is realization of Truth *as us.* You will note something special going on here as you identify: you are not denying or affirming anymore — you are presently conscious of I AM. For reference I would like to bring your thought to the poem on *Presence* from *The Bridge.* In the last two lines the important thing that is brought out is that the I AM with capital letters is the I am with lower case letters, one and the same thing.

> Feeling such Oneness I pause
> and know the full effect:
> I AM,
> and I am Cause.[33]

---

31. *S. & H.* 325:27-29
32. *Mis.* 331:26-28
33. *The Bridge,* poem on pages 142 and 143.

The I AM is assuredly your divine nature, including all the purpose and fulfillment as you. Why should we accept this understanding? Because it gives us spiritual authority in every situation. It gives meaning and direction to our lives, assuring us of the ever-presence of God-in-Us, Principle, Mind, Soul, Spirit, Life, Truth, Love, all substance, intelligence governing and explaining our every activity, establishing in us a conscious state of joy and well-being. There is tremendous energizing power expressed in the statement I have just quoted from *Miscellaneous Writings*. We are not going to allow the I AM to be something separate from us called "Deity." Let *us* be that which is Deity— the I AM—because I AM contains all qualities of Mind (Deity).

I do *not* mean we go around saying we are God, in the sense of the creator or the sovereign of the universe. That is not the thought we have when we say we are Principle or Deity, the I AM. We have learned the qualitative aspects of God through our study and instruction of Christian Science, and in the higher order of Science we show them forth in our lives as serenity, confidence, rationality, unjudgmental concepts of Man and our Universe, always demonstrating the Love which is God, the Mind which is God, and, of course, all the other attributes of Godliness. This consciousness is our God-Being-Us. By identifying as Godliness (Godlikeness), or to the point of that divine Oneness, we put the I AM into our daily lives, and I mean moment-by-moment. Our God-Being-Love is seen and felt in every contact in which we are placed. Many are the opportunities we have to be this Principle in operation. In other words, when you read that "Divine Love has strengthened the hand and encouraged the heart of every member of this large church . . . [and] hath opened the gate Beautiful to us, where we may see God and live, see good in good,—God all, one,—one Mind and that divine . . ."[34] you know that that divine Love is the essence of your very own divinity.

In the *Unity of Good* chapter on *The Saviour's Mission,* we find Mrs. Eddy speaking of Christ as the I AM. She declares that Christ as "The I AM was neither buried nor resurrected. The Way, the Truth and the Life were never absent for a moment." [35] From this we have an authority for seeing the I AM as not restricted to a God separate from *our* Being anymore than the I AM was separated from Jesus, the Christ. As the I AM we are in unity with Truth and Life. The account of Jesus' burial and resurrection was a fulfillment of prophecy. As the Messiah he carried out all that was predestined for him. So we, identifying as the I AM, have the opportunity to go beyond the historical account of Jesus' experiences. We hold to the continuity of Life, the immortality of the *I AM THAT I AM* for ourselves. We glory in our Christ ascension. This is the higher order of Life applied to us in today's understanding of Being. Dare to make these thoughts your own:

> ". . . I am ever-conscious Life . . ."[36]
> "I am ALL."[37]
> "Mind is the I AM, or infinity."[38]

---

34. *My.* 132:16-21
35. *Un.* 63:2-4
36. *Un.* 18:23
37. *Un.* 18:25
38. *S. & H.* 336:1-2

And with this spiritual courage of conscious identity have your own wonderful inspiring unfoldment. I just received an interesting letter today from a Christian Scientist, and I would like to quote it. She says: "One time when I was trying to resolve a problem the old hymn *Rock of Ages* began to run through my mind this way: 'Rock of Ages, cleft for me, let me *find* [not hide] myself in Thee'." And she adds, "I did." Our spiritual identity *finds* itself *as* Truth, *as* Mind, *as* I AM and in doing this it changes and deletes whatever is outgrown.

In *S. & H.*, 290:1-2, we read, "Life is the everlasting I AM, the Being who was and is and shall be, whom nothing can erase." Do you think this is a reference limited to God? Why surely you know this refers to *you* "whom nothing can erase." *Your* life is the everlasting I AM! Orthodox students reading this believe that God is the only ". . . Being who was and is and shall be . . ." They do not dare to identify themselves as everlasting Life. Yet, this is the work Mrs. Eddy expected her students to do in the higher order of Christian Science. We are to recognize, to identify ourselves as Life itself in a most natural and normal way, and I must say in an all-inclusive way, such that the God, I AM, is ". . . at once the center and circumference of being." [39] Whose being? *Yours.*

Here is a letter from one who is identifying with the higher order of Spirit and Mind. She writes: "I just read, 'Spirit exists in thought; it is not objectified.' Now I don't agree with that statement. I think it does exist and it *is* objectified . . . I am Spirit (individuality)

39. *S. & H.* 203:32 to 204:1

in manifestation. I am Mind in manifestation, too; otherwise how would you know Spirit or Mind???" I do not know what she was quoting but a least she was challenging this statement wherever she found it, and she was translating it for herself.

Yes, *you* are the Mind that is ". . . the I AM, or infinity." This statement is found in the chapter in *S. & H.* on the *Science of Being. You* are this Science, and in knowing this you express it in your present, daily life in all its flexibility and variation. In other words *live* the following statement as a person knowing that "The divine Ego, or individuality, is reflected [expressed] in all spiritual individuality from the infinitesimal to the infinite." [10] *Your* Ego; *your* individuality.

Richard Bach, author of *Jonathan Livingston Seagull,*[41] dedicates his book "To the real Jonathan Seagull, who lives within us all." One of the reasons for the book's popularity may be that those who read it identify with its metaphysical ideas and are carried away with flight into the infinite. In a moment of awareness Jonathan identifies with all that is happening to him and says, "Why, that's true! I *am* a perfect, unlimited gull!" What a great joy he felt! This is what we experience in our identification as the I AM: perfection, infinite, boundless bliss! We read in Bach's book:

> Each of us is in truth an idea of the Great Gull, an unlimited idea of freedom . . .

What Chiang had taught Jonathan was that there was no limit to Being. And Jonathan taught it to

---

40. *S. & H.* 336:6-8
41. Richard Bach: *Jonathan Livingston Seagull,* The Macmillan Co., 1970, pp. 27, 59, 76, 93.

Fletcher, *his* student. Fletcher got the message and when he was about to teach his first class we note this in the last sentence of the book:

> . . . Fletcher Seagull suddenly saw them all as they really were, just for a moment, and he more than liked, he loved what it was he saw. No limits, Jonathan? he thought, and he smiled. His race to learn had begun.

Truly, in the higher order of Identity we are the Mind, the I AM, the actual, the potential, the infinite. This Mind is our strength, our perception, our substance, our being. It is our infinite activity, our supply, our intelligence and our love. It enters into every detail of our lives and we, too, possess an awareness of an abiding consciousness of infinite capability. Jonathan says, "We can lift ourselves out of ignorance, we can find ourselves as creatures of excellence and intelligence and skill. We can be free! We can learn to fly!"

———————

Now that I have explained how you identify as Mind in its higher order, how are you going to evaluate statements in *S. & H.* and *Prose Works* which you find difficult to accept because you are now understanding Science in its greater meaning? Just remember this: *you are going to translate them.* This means you are going to bring them up to a clearer acceptance because you have outgrown them as they are. You are your own authority now; you are spiritually independent and you are going to translate from the premise that "All is infinite Mind, and its infinite manifestation, for God is All-in-all." Remember the last letter I read to you—and also remember this: because of the infinite expression of spiritual individuality various translations are not necessarily alike. Each one does this work for himself; he is his own seer and prophet, his own physician, his interpreter, his Christ.

Using our premise, let's consider this reference from *S. & H.* 91:16-17: "Absorbed in material selfhood we discern and reflect but faintly the substance of Life or Mind." First of all, how shall we define "material selfhood"? It is something we used to consider error. Why? Because it includes just about all our activities, living in the flesh as we do, surrounded with the many material objects, pursuits and interests. Each personal interest may be defined as "material selfhood" in orthodox Christian Science — just my sitting here typing, or feeding the birds, or getting groceries, driving my car, answering the telephone, taking care of correspondence — even my reading this address. Is one spiritual only when he is at church meetings, or reading Christian Science literature, doing the Lesson, singing hymns or contemplating a world of spiritual ideas? Surely his spirituality cannot be so limited. Why, we have just been identifying ourselves as the I AM! Material selfhood, then, is to be recognized as the spirituality of one's self. As a matter of fact this "material selfhood" was the form in which Mrs. Eddy lived and worked when she wrote *S. & H.* through the reading of which we are often aroused to great ideas, not discerning "faintly" but understanding quite clearly that this "material selfhood" is in reality the divine.

A woman who read *The Bridge* understood this when

she wrote the following letter to me: "No need to feel guilty for taking part in the activities of the family, the community, or even in pursuing special interests." She also wrote, "Yes, I will let the peace and serenity and wholeness constitute my being, and love and enjoy my being at all times from the premise of Allness."

Advancing in Christian Science the student knows his life to be *expressing* his personal individuality, his divinity, his true selfhood all the time, and he knows that this selfhood expands and grows as *material/ spiritual* selfhood, a glorious I AM.

Having just written the word "glorious" reminds me of the wonderful book, *The Wilderness World of John Muir*.[42] In the introduction we read this: "There have been those who have complained, with some basis, that Muir's books tended to be 'adjectivorous,' that all his mountain streams 'sang psalms,' that he overworked such words as 'glorious.' . . . Muir himself was aware of his fondness for certain adjectives and wrote to his friend Robert Underwood Johnson of *Century Maga- zine* that he had been slaughtering 'gloriouses' in his manuscript. However, his overworking of this adjec- tive was, in itself, a key to his character. For him, always, the world *was* glorious." Let us not hesitate to identify with this word, seeing our universe *as it is* in all its glorious manifestation of Mind.

As one resolves the person/personality dilemma which has surrounded him in orthodoxy he discovers great things, among them a marvelous concept of ge- neric man as his own infinite selfhood. Consider with

---

42. Edwin Way Teale: *The Wilderness World of John Muir*. Houghton Mifflin Co., Boston, Mass. 1954, p. XV.

me for a moment a few things about yourself: To your parents you are still a child, to your child, a parent; to a husband you are a wife, and to a wife you are a husband. To a neighbor you are a friend, to the postman you are someone to whom he delivers mail. To a niece you are an aunt, maybe an uncle. You may be a grandfather, a mother, a teacher, an employer—and this goes on infinitely when you consider generic man in this way. How infinite you are as spiritual individuality! Each has his place in the marvelous universe of Life, and a very important place, too. Accept your place, live it vitally, lovingly and all-inclusively as "I AM ALL," accepting your material selfhood as your spiritual being and Christ-consciousness, *one and the same thing!* This is the grand identification that every practitioner sees as Mind before it comes into view as form and substance. You are your own practitioner; you identify; you see Mind in every manifestation!

For many years this poem has been meaningful to me, and I feel that here I have an appropriate place to record it.

THE BUILDERS

> All are architects of Fate,
>   Working in these walls of Time;
> Some with massive deeds and great,
>   Some with ornaments of rhyme.
>
> Nothing useless is, or low;
>   Each thing in its place is best;
> And what seems but idle show
>   Strengthens and supports the rest.[43]

---

43. *The Complete Poetical Works of Longfellow,* Houghton Mifflin Co., Boston, Mass., 1922, p. 108.

Since I do not believe that ". . . human history needs to be revised, and the material record expunged,"[44] I am going to tell you a little bit about my own material history. There is no better place to start than from a little diary written when I was 16 years old, living in New York City attending High School. It is not incidental that I chose a poem by Alexander Pope to be the first thing to appear in it. It is *Essay on Man,* and although I wrote out nine couplets I shall include here only four of them.

> Know then thyself; presume not God to scan.
> The proper study of Mankind is Man.
>
> *　*　*　*
>
> Hope springs eternal in the human breast.
> Man never is but always to be blest.
>
> *　*　*　*
>
> All are but parts of one stupendous whole
> Whose body nature is and God the Soul.
>
> *　*　*　*
>
> Honor and shame from no conditions rise.
> Act well your part. There all the honor lies.

In this same diary, a year and a half later, I was to write my first thoughts about Christian Science. I record them exactly as they are written in the book:

> I am becoming very interested in Christian
> Science. After all, to have beautiful thoughts
> of that which we think unbeautiful. To find

---

44. *Ret.* 22:1-2

out that we are really living in an unreal state of Mind and in reality that only reigns love, peace, understanding where there is no sickness, no physical ailments, to be healed by beautiful thoughts. Is it not the truth which I have been seeking these 17 years? Perhaps I have found it at last in Christian Science.

I have found a God—my God is Love, Mind, always present, divine supreme. It is as though I were awakened up out of a long sleep realizing that I have lived too long in that dream, too long in a state of unreality.

My aim is to walk in the footsteps of our Leader, Mrs. Baker Eddy, to have the mind that was also in Christ Jesus, to demonstrate that Mind is all—Mind over matter—to know that sin, sickness and death are unreal for God is the opposite, health, Life which is Truth.

We hear the Truth in many different places. I first heard about Christian Science in a department store in New York City. Two women were standing near me at a counter and, fortunately, were talking very loudly. They were talking about a healing and I heard them use the words "Christian Science." It was the first time I ever heard it mentioned. I was so inquisitive I asked them a few questions right there and then. They told me they had just come from a noon-hour service at Town Hall and had heard several testimonies of healing. My interest became very much increased.

Although we were going to a Protestant Church at the time my parents finally enrolled me in the Christian Science Sunday School at my request. They thought that in a short time I would return with them to attend their church. But it was not a teenager's whim that took me into the new Sunday School. I was making a serious commitment of identification with Christian Science. Subsequently my interest in Christian Science developed to the point that in later years it became a devoted and absorbing occupation fulfilling the hopes I had when I was a young girl. In the same diary, after listing my occupation and my aims in life, I wrote on its first page, "I have great expectations of becoming a teacher." May I thank you all now for being part of this fulfillment.

———

Not long ago I was visiting a patient in her home. With all my reassurances of her spirituality she hesitated to identify with her divine nature. Every time I spoke of something of a spiritual nature as part of her own identity she would say, "But that is God; that is not me." She had no knowledge of *The Bridge,* and I thought before leaving I might introduce it to her. In my work with her I noticed that she was preferring to recognize the God-consciousness as something far removed and outside of herself. She reminded me that her teacher warned his students they must *never* identify with "I AM," that this was strictly a reference to and for Deity. She showed me this: "The name, I AM, indicated no personality that could be paralleled with it; but it did declare a mighty individuality . . ."[45] I

———

45. *Mis.* 258:21-23

spoke to her about Mrs. Eddy relating the I AM to Christ Jesus, a man walking around in the flesh, a man who ate with his disciples, who prepared breakfast for them, who bathed his disciples' feet, and healed the sick,—but it did not move her. Her understanding was kept in the frozen form of the letter and she preferred to remain like Moses, afraid to see her own divinity as the revelation of her spiritual self. She seemed so fixed on her mortality, her humanness, with the many references to mortal mind and to herself in such a deprecating way, that I felt she should be lovingly directed back to the Lesson-Sermons, realizing that she still had work to do within the instruction before she would be willing to accept a higher order for her divinity.

On the other hand, consider with me the pure inspiration that came to the Mr. Hudson who is quoted in *S. & H.* page 669, referred to in *The Bridge* on pages 254-255. Mr. Hudson's experience brought him into the infinite meaning of the "I." He trod, as it were, on holy ground in that he became intelligently conscious of the ever-presence of an infinite God. In other words, he went into the depth of his spiritual nature and within it found himself.

This same great discovery is described in a book called *The Man Who Tapped The Secrets Of The Universe*, by Glenn Clark. It is the story of the life of Walter Russell, a sculptor, who identified with a spiritual force that was governing his every thought and action. I quote the following from his book to show that this identification of God-Being within is admitted by others outside the Christian Science organization. "If one interprets the God within one, one's thoughts

and actions must be balanced rhythmic waves." In
his life philosophy this principle is stated as follows:
"I will see beauty and goodness in all things." He states
on page 43:

> Many have asked if I could more specifically
> direct them to kindle that spark of inner fire
> which illumines the way to one's self. That I
> cannot do. I can merely point the way and
> tell you of its existence. You must then find it
> yourself. The only way you can find it is
> through being alone with your thoughts at
> sufficiently long intervals to give that inner
> voice within you a chance to cry out in dis-
> tinguishable language to you, 'Here I am
> within you.' That is the silent voice of nature,
> which speaks to everyone who will listen . . .
> All knowledge exists in the God-Mind . . .
> all you have to do is to recollect it, or recog-
> nize it, for you already have it as your inherit-
> ance.[46]

Here in this following statement you recognize the
Higher Order: "The Scripture declares that God is
All. Then all is Spirit and spiritual."[47] Surely if there
is no place without God/Spirit, then all is Spirit or
all is made up of Spirit or all there *is* is Spirit, and
this would include what we call matter. On the other
hand, you may come to a statement like this: "When
the substance of Spirit appears in Christian Science,

46. Glenn Clark: *The Man Who Tapped The Secrets of The Universe,*
Macalester Park Publishers, 1969, pp. 31, 43.

47. *My.* 178:12-13

the nothingness of matter is recognized."[48] And if you do, you instantly recognize this as an orthodox attempt to annihilate matter, to deny what is really formulated Spirit. All we have, truthfully, is *Spirit,* the Mind that is all, the all that is mind, and matter is part of its great design.

Several years ago, at a time when I was questioning many things, I came upon the following statement which epitomized for me what seemed then to be an impassable gulf between Spirit and matter:

> Spirit is the only substance, the invisible and indivisible infinite God. Things spiritual and eternal arc substantial. Things material and temporal are insubstantial.[49]

Today, I must lovingly challenge the claims of this paragraph from *Science and Health.* It is clear to me that what constitutes our world is in Truth and in substance all that we behold. Call it matter, beauty, nature or any other name, it is substance *itself* that we are viewing. Do we have to continue thinking of it as something temporal and insubstantial while the real things of Spirit are invisible to us? What good is this concept of Spirit as substance if we cannot see it, or hear it or feel its effect in some way? There is no point in postponing our appreciation of good things as they materially are for the spiritual things that arc so intangible. We live today, and today we know the reality of Spirit to be rightfully understood as our experience. Is everything I handle or see or hear some-

48. *S. & H.* 480:1-2
49. *S. & H.* 335:12-15

thing to deprecate because it is of form or of sight or
sound? If this is the case, then where and when do we
begin to magnify the spiritual and eternal things that
are substantial? I know that *these things are now,* and
my identification with them is a present one. They
actually are the glory and majesty of my Spirit/sense
experience, and they are yours as well as you identify
these objects of sense as objects of soul. Let me quote
from another interesting letter I received since writing *The Bridge*:

> . . . how comforting it is to read something
> that another one has written and find the
> mental experience so similar that it comforts
> by being able to read it 'spelled out.' And I
> marvel at the ability to trace each thought out
> to its explanation by comparison or justifica-
> tion according to all writings. I can frankly
> say that I never was in agreement with the
> dualistic presentation and as the fifty years
> have gone along, never have been able to re-
> solve the frustration that has continued all
> through the desire, determination and patient
> willingness to try to find the answer. With
> HOPE always, because of the Science of Be-
> ing, I continued.

This woman identified with some of the thoughts in
The Bridge which illustrate the Higher Order—and
she reached a peace and a feeling of Oneness she had
not had before.

Now, as a last quotation in the group I have taken

from Mrs. Eddy's writings I want to give you one that recapitulates the orthodoxy in all of them:

> . . . when we subordinate the false testimony of the corporeal senses to the facts of Science, we shall see this true likeness and reflection everywhere.[50]

I think you can understand what a great revelation it was to me when I realized that all I had to do was to accept and *see* the true likeness of substance everywhere. There was no need to be subordinating ". . . the false testimony of the corporeal senses . . ." at all because what I had been terming "false testimony" through the instruction of orthodox Christian Science was the substance of the real in the higher order of Science all the time. It is, in fact, the evidence of Spirit, the proof of Spirit's grand and glorious existence as the world of events.

In contrast to the quote just mentioned Mrs. Eddy expresses recognition of this higher order of Matter in all its glory in the paragraph on page 516:9-23 of *Science and Health*. Notice that she speaks of the grass, the modest arbutus, the great rock, the sunlight, flowers, landscape, and earth, and she continues right up to man and woman reflecting (expressing) ". . . in glorified quality, the infinite Father-Mother God." All this she sees as something wonderful. Why, may we ask, did she feel she had to ". . . *subordinate the false testimony of the corporeal senses* . . ." and expect it of the members of her church as well? In the higher order

---

50. *S. & H.* 516:6-8

of Christian Science our corporeal senses see all these things in their true likeness, and we love what we see: *Spirit.*

———

As I go on with references I think I should stop to explain what I mean by translation. It is taking a statement to the highest interpretation of Mind, *your* Mind, no matter what authority is given. You know you are your own authority as far as interpretation is concerned, and with this, your own illumination, your discovery and revelation are known to you. Remember, there may be many different interpretations of statements, but you have a right to make your own according to your highest understanding.

Here is a reference we can use to illustrate how we translate:

> The everlasting I AM is not bounded nor compressed within the narrow limits of physical humanity, nor can He be understood aright through mortal concepts.[51]

First of all, correct the marginal heading so that it reads "Divine Corporeality" instead of "No divine corporeality." You know now that the word corporeality contains *reality* within it (look at the word) and you realize also that the infinite I AM accepts no boundaries. Of course the Christ, *your* everlasting I AM, is not ". . . compressed within . . . narrow limits . . ." of any kind, for your recognition of physi-

———

51. *S. & H.* 256:13-16

cal humanity as really spiritual humanity takes away what appear to be limits. Then the "He" which is the I AM of us understands "mortal concepts" perfectly through the translation we have given them. They are really the divine concepts forever at hand blessing us in every conceivable way.

In other words, if physicality is such an unfortunate thing (as is implied many times in the orthodox point of view) our work is to raise it to its proper status as our higher order of Humanity. If you find it difficult to be this scientific at all times then at least be as philosophical as the Russian peasant, Karataev, who utters these words in Tolstoy's *War and Peace*:[52]

> 'And have you seen a lot of trouble, sir? Eh?' said the little man suddenly. And there was a tone of such friendliness and simplicity in the sing-song voice that Pierre wanted to answer, but his jaw quivered, and he felt the tears rising. At the same second, leaving no time for Pierre's embarrassment to appear, the little man said, in the same pleasant voice: 'Ay, darling, don't grieve,' he said, in that tender, caressing sing-song in which old Russian peasant women talk. 'Don't grieve, dearie; trouble lasts an hour, but life lasts forever!'

Yes. We fulfill our *humanness* as we understand it to be our *spirituality*. The concept of Oneness *has to include these two* or there is no validity to it. Our Christ-consciousness gives us grander, more acceptable

52. Leo Tolstoy: *War and Peace.* The Modern Library Edition, Random House, New York, N.D. p. 910.

views of our physical humanity. We neither destroy it, misunderstand it, nor limit it. We lift everything up through translation to its highest potential.

In the preface to *Prose Works* by Mary Baker Eddy, she writes on page xi, "May this volume be to the reader a graphic guidebook, pointing the path, dating the unseen, and enabling him to walk the untrodden in the hitherto unexplored fields of Science." My invitation to students is to identify with more of this Science in its higher order, knowing through living and loving the present awareness of celestial Being.

Identify with your own celestial Being as you read this poem written in the 16th Century by Thomas Traherne, and remember: everyone here today has the grand privilege of saying "That's me."

WONDER

How like an Angel came I down!
 How bright are all things here!
When first among His works I did appear
 Oh how their glory me did crown!

The world resembled His Eternity,
 In which my soul did walk;
And every thing that I did see
 Did with me talk.

The skies in their magnificence,
 The lively, lovely air,
Oh how divine, how soft, how sweet, how fair!
 The stars did entertain my sense,
And all the works of God, so bright and pure,
 So rich and great did seem,

As if they ever must endure
   In my esteem.

A native health and innocence
   Within my bones did grow,
And while my God did all his Glories show,
   I felt a vigour in my sense
That was all Spirit. I within did flow
   With seas of life, like wine;
I nothing in the world did know
   But 'twas divine.

Harsh ragged objects were concealed,
   Oppressions, tears and cries,
Sins, griefs, complaints, dissensions, weeping eyes
   Were hid, and only things revealed
Which heavenly Spirits and Angels prize.
   The state of Innocence
And bliss, not trades and poverties
   Did fill my sense.

The streets were paved with golden stones
   The boys and girls were mine,
Oh, how did all their lovely faces shine!
   The sons of men were holy ones,
In joy and beauty they appeared to me
   And every thing which here I found,
While like an Angel I did see,
   Adorned the ground.

Rich diamond and pearl and gold
   In every place was seen;
Rare splendours, yellow, blue, red, white and green,
   Mine eyes did everywhere behold.

Great wonders clothed with glory did appear,
    Amazement was my bliss,
That and my wealth was everywhere;
    No joy to this!

Cursed and devised properties,
    With envy, avarice
And fraud, those fiends that spoil even Paradise,
    Flew from the splendour of mine eyes,
And so did hedges, ditches, limits, bounds,
    I dreamed not aught of those,
But wandered over all men's grounds,
    And found repose.

Properties themselves were mine,
    And hedges ornaments;
Walls, boxes, coffers, and their rich contents
    Did not divine my joys, but all combine.
Clothes, ribbons, jewels, laces, I esteemed
    My joys by others worn:
For me they all to wear them seemed
    When I was born.[53]

In *Misc. Writings*, page 258, we read ". . . God named Himself, I AM." And in the highest sense of Soul as our divine character and spiritual individuality we name ourselves, I AM.

––––––––––

I would like now to talk about the man at the pool who had had an infirmity thirty-eight years. He was

––––––––––

53. *The Oxford Book of English Mystical Verse.* Oxford, At the Clarendon Press, 1953. pp. 63, 64 and 65.

waiting for the moving of the waters and for many other things to happen in order to be healed of his affliction. Jesus knew that he did not have to treat the man's infirmity. He went directly to the heart of the matter, asking him if he wanted to be made whole. Oh, yes, he wanted that more than anything, but his own excuses got in the way, and they had accumulated for such a long time that he finally believed them, but when Jesus told him to take up his bed and walk, he did so.

This command to rise was not only directed toward the performance of a physical act but it was a spiritual acknowledgment as well. May I ask you: Do you think it was a spiritual body that rose, a body so spiritual that it could not be seen as physical form? Wasn't the spiritual rise of consciousness accompanied by that man physically getting up and walking around? Surely this man at the pool had been absorbed in his "material selfhood" for a long time and just as surely he had not been subordinating ". . . the false testimony of the corporeal senses to the facts of Science." But *Jesus saw the Oneness of Man before him* and he was not concerned with anything else than the wholeness of this man's being. The material man sitting at the pool was the spiritual man all the time, even though *he* himself had not known it. Jesus *did* know it, however, and he introduced this man to a higher order of his Identity as a physical/spiritual self that was not as limited as he had thought it to be. In this healing there was no disappearance of corporeal sense to this man; there was in fact a grander appearance of it in that his bodily strength was restored to him. Life came at once to his senses and his senses came to Life!

Let us this day accept our divine nature as our person; let us live it objectively and subjectively as I AM.

Please review pages 102 through 105 in *The Bridge* where I go into the definition of God and end the thought with this quotation from Meister Eckhart: ". . . where I am there is God, and where God is there I am." Also read page 350 of *The Bridge* beginning with "This vital feeling . . ." and ending on page 351 with the words ". . . Old Testament."

In our home, when I was a young girl, we had a painting of Daniel in the lion's den. I regarded it then as just a religious painting, perhaps also having some historical interest, but that was all. I *did* know, however, that I was very impressed with one thing about Daniel: it was his apparent indifference to the presence of the lions. He was believing and trusting his knowledge of God. It took courage to do this and his awareness of his God-consciousness gave it to him.

When the king found that the lions had not harmed Daniel he was taken up and out of the den. ". . . no manner of hurt was found upon him, *because he believed in his God.*"[54] It is clear that Daniel, humanly, was the same person when he came out as when he went in. He was a physical being, a corporeal mortal, a man who ". . . believed in his God." This means he had faith in his own goodness; it means he understood his spiritual nature, yet in this understanding he was moving about in a material form just as you and I. The important thing about the story to me is that he *identified himself as Spirit in his physicality,*

---

54. *Daniel* 6:23 (Italics mine).

and not only did he see this for himself but *he saw it for the lions as well!* Actually, when you think of it in this light, it was his conception of a higher order of Matter that saved him. He did not "misconceive" himself or the lions; he did not see them as illusions. He saw them as they were: perfect in their spiritual/ physicality. He saw as his God-Spirit sees and with this perfect vision there was nothing to harm him.

When we refer to Mrs. Eddy's thought on lions in *Rudimental Divine Science,* 8:4-6, we read: "To sense, the lion of to-day is the lion of six thousand years ago; but in Science, Spirit sends forth its own harmless likeness." We translate the first part of this statement and we hold to the Scientific concept in the second. Then we have our lion lying down with the lamb.

What importance would the story of Daniel have to us if it had no direct bearing on our own lives? We may be placed in situations that are not always as comfortable as they should be. It really does not matter what the circumstances are; we immediately identify with our spiritual nature, our understanding of the divine power within us. We hold consistently to our spiritual integrity and we endow the circumstances facing us with the same goodness of Spirit, knowing always that "The divine understanding reigns, is *all,* and there is no other consciousness."[55] In my practice I find that when I am able to get a patient to stop ruminating about his problem (which he wants to be free of anyway) it is then possible for me to lead him to the realization of his divine consciousness within, whereupon the real work, the reality of his Being, takes

---

55. *S. & H.* 536:8-9

over and he is at peace. It is all done by showing him to himself as a new image, a recognition of himself as Truth.

I would like to share several stories you may have already heard, but they are, I feel, worth repeating because of our work on Identity. One is about a woman who visited a practitioner regarding a physical problem she had. She went on relating how very miserable she was and how limited was her strength to cope with her situation. The practitioner asked her to say, "I am omnipotent!" She said she could not do that because such a statement could be made only by God. "Well," the practitioner said, "just go ahead and feel the power of the word and say it anyway." She hesitated for a long time, but finally said it and then repeated it as her understanding took hold. She was instantaneously healed, and in her healing she was aroused to a new feeling about herself, and her situation. She had identified as *spiritual power*.

Then there is the story of a man who told his practitioner about the trouble he was having with his business associates. They were deprecating his ability and were calling him names that were not complimentary. The practitioner asked him if they were calling him the Son of God! He said they certainly were not. The practitioner said, "Then they are not talking about you." This story has meaning for all of us. Once we have accepted a higher order for our identity, and we live it, we never need to be concerned about what is being said about us, for living the highest we know is itself satisfying and fulfilling. It brings to us the perfect peace we deserve.

The third story is about another man who was having a difficult time with the people in his office. He needed to have a better relationship with them, more harmony. He told his practitioner how this one and that one needed to be changed and that he felt so many people were involved he did not know where to begin. The practitioner said, "Which one needs to express more harmony?" The patient immediately got the message. He knew that only *one* needed to express harmony and that *one* was himself.

These three stories point up the importance of identifying correctly in a situation. It makes for wonderful happenings. You may recall the song that was written a few years ago: "Let there be peace on earth, and let it begin with me." Yes, let the peace, the love, the understanding of our true natures begin with us.

May we now turn our thought to the first part of the definition of *Ark,* found in the *Glossary* of *Science and Health.* Let's give it a new interpretation, but first a portion of the definition as it is written:

> ARK. Safety; the idea, or reflection, of Truth, proved to be as immortal as its Principle; the understanding of Spirit, destroying belief in matter.[56]

We all know the account of Noah's experience. In spite of Mrs. Eddy's opinion of him ("A corporeal mortal; knowledge of the nothingness of material

---

56. *S. & H.* 581:8-10

things . . .") we must conclude that it was Noah's *higher understanding of mortality* that saved the human race and the animal kingdom, for he was instructed to take into the Ark his family as well as a male and female of each animal species. This understanding of preservation committed him to the spiritual fact that Truth's immortality required the material concepts, the corporeality of people and animals, and his function was to preserve these concepts. The ark was the spiritual/material idea of safety. If Noah had questioned the instruction he received on the grounds that animals were mortal concepts, material illusions, or misconceptions of Truth, as we understand them to be in orthodox Christian Science, he might not have gone about his God-directed business. But he, too, like Daniel, ". . . believed in his God." He had a spiritual understanding of immortality within the framework of mortality, and he followed out the orders given to him. Destroying beliefs in matter means translating the traditional idea of matter as "bad" into its real identity, Spirit.

Think with me about this quotation from the definition for a moment: "The ark indicates temptation overcome and followed by exaltation." This is the orthodox interpretation of Ark but the correct translation sees it as a material/spiritual idea of Love. Thus any thought that it could be anything but Godly is removed and in this light there could have been no temptation to overcome! This wonderful man, Noah, defined in our textbook, is given to us to study in our Lesson-Sermons as,

NOAH. A corporeal mortal; knowledge of the nothingness of material things and of the immortality of all that is spiritual.[57]

We should not hesitate to have a new authority about Noah in the higher order of Science. As a corporeal mortal he *did not accept "the nothingness of material things"* at all! He saw something wonderful in them, in material man and in the animals, as well as in the Ark itself. To him, his material universe was beautiful! And because of his higher acceptance of material things he performed an activity that preserved the continuity of all of us! In a marvelous way he saw life going on in the presence of Love. We must never forget that it was his identity as a spiritual *corporeal mortal* that functioned so obediently, lovingly and intelligently. Refuse to be taken in by the idea that a corporeal mortal is erroneous! Translate this thought. Discover the divinity of everyone in his corporeality and glorify it.

The definition of God in the *Glossary* defines Principle as one of its great synonyms. In *Misc. Writings*, 117:1-3, Mrs. Eddy states what she understands a progressive life to be and she defines it in terms of Principle as follows:

A progressive life is the reality of Life that unfolds its immortal principle.

---

57. *S. & H.* 592:22-24

Now this "Life" is meaningless to us within our present framework unless we identify with it. Therefore we recognize that the life she is writing about is *our* life — the immortal Principle unfolding to us in a remarkably wondrous way. Surely we do not have to die out of mortality to experience this immortal Principle; our lives are progressive, enjoying Reality now. The higher order of Life is that understanding which reveals our *present* immortality to us.

When Jesus stated "Before Abraham was, I am," he was declaring his identity as Principle. Even though his experience as the Messiah was of short duration he knew his existence to be eternal and forever *in its totality*. His pronouncement that if his body were destroyed he would lift it up in three days was a statement of the grand continuity of his life, a constant progression unfolding his immortal Principle. For us, Mrs. Eddy sums it up beautifully when she states: "If we live after death and are immortal, we must have lived before birth . . ." [58] Students usually do not pay much attention to this reference because it brings up the question of reincarnation and they wish to avoid such thoughts — but the statement does profess an assumption of our eternal existence. And, of course, if we accept its full meaning we cannot accept another of Mrs. Eddy's statements about ". . . man as never born and as never dying . . ." (*S. & H.* 557:20-21). In *The Bridge,* page 113, I write, "Let your own divinity assert itself and proclaim its authority where you are. Let us see each person as having an immortal birth, an immortal Being brought into view. You, man, person, are

---

58. *S. & H.* 429:21-22

visible, and immortality is part of this vision." Birth is proof of self-existence; death declares Life! So, you always are visible to someone in the eternal existence of your divinity.

To hold on to this immortal identity I repeat: Jesus knew he lived before Abraham and he knew he would live after the crucifixion. We lose the full import of this if we limit it to the spiritual idea, the Christ, as apart from Jesus, the person. Remember that *Jesus was speaking as a mortal when he announced his immortality*. We do not hesitate to speak our highest concept of Truth in our mortality because we have given our mortality its own spiritual distinction. Let us say that through the scientific work of translation we see our mortality raised to its high status, its immortal form and structure.

It is important to understand that the higher order of Life is our present immortal Principle living us just as it was living Jesus. Willing approval of Principle living us takes away all kinds of fears, for in our acknowledgment that we are in a reality that is part of the great continuum called "life" we accept our foreverness.

Now here is some correspondence from one who is allowing his immortal Principle to unfold in a hospital. In his first letter he writes to me: "My dear and glorious physician came to see me yesterday and told me that while I was having medication that would slow my heart down there might be some unpleasant side effects. The next day, since no side effects had occurred, the doctor remarked, 'Who do *you* know? You seem to be so much improved, I can't believe it.' I said, 'Well, you call him the man upstairs, but I call him God-Being-Here-*You*.' He looked at me for a second and said, 'I'm going to do something I've never done before in my life.' Then he kissed me on the cheek, saying, 'God bless you'." Soon after the first, a second letter followed and it read: "The other night I covered my head and began to cry and a doctor came by. He pulled off the covers and asked why I was crying. I said, 'I was not crying. I was just watering the seeds of gratitude in my heart.' As he walked away he must have thought I had flipped." These experiences are spiritually profitable as illustrations of the continual unfolding of God-consciousness wherever we are. We learn more and more that this inevitable progression of Life is going on in a hospital as well as in a practitioner's office. Life walks the street, sees *Superstar,* visits a friend, reads the scriptures, digs a ditch, polishes the silver, sings a hymn.

Many times I have turned to the definition of Abraham in the *Glossary,* knowing that what was true for him must be true for me. In divine moments of awareness I identified with the qualities of fidelity and faithfulness such as I knew him to have. I was growing a more expansive purpose of Love in my own experience, and certainly I was creating more trust in God, good. I knew that Love had showed me the life-preserving power of my own spiritual understanding, and that if it were shown to me, it must be shown as Truth for each and every one. Love shows us many things as our spiritual understanding matures into the divine Principle we are.

In my early practice of Christian Science I felt on some occasions that I might not have sufficient faith to demonstrate Christian healing. But whenever I read the definition of *Abraham* it became clear that the qualities expressed for him were the very qualities I needed to accept for myself and for my universe. It was of tremendous value as I let myself *identify*. Through the years I have reminded students of this definition, as well as many others, and have asked them to make their own identification. Here it is:

ABRAHAM. Fidelity; faith in the divine Life and in the eternal Principle of being. This patriarch illustrated the purpose of Love to create trust in good, and showed the life-preserving power of spiritual understanding.[59]

The chapter in *The Bridge* titled *Man, Present Being,* was written to clarify the fact that when we read about Man in the Bible or in *Science and Health* or *Prose Works,* or in any other metaphysical book stating the Truth, we have the grand, spiritual opportunity to identify ourselves with the higher order of ourselves. And I must add here that it is about time to do this important work, for through the instruction of orthodoxy we have been indoctrinated with the belief we are mortal and therefore have been born in sin, with all its uncomplimentary images and meanings. It is

---

59. *S. & H.* 579:10-14

really a matter of "Choose ye this day whom thou shalt serve." Will it be a higher order of your Science or will you hold to the ritual of services which keep you forever bound with their dualism?

In seeing, feeling and knowing that today all there is to us is Principle operating as our divinity, our daily lives express order, harmony of being, peace, fullness of joy, absolute goodness, creativity and so many other manifestations of Mind. Should you want to know yourself as Man, Principle, read *Misc. Writings,* pages 147:14-30, accepting this man as the higher order of Identity for yourself. You are the "man of integrity" she is talking about. Then it follows that "When understood, Principle is found to be the only term that fully conveys the ideas of God, — one Mind, a perfect man, and divine Science." [60] It should be clear by now that we are always working with higher ideas within ourselves because we identify with these ideas. It used to be that whenever we were *working with* Principle we would be inclined to shy away from ever allowing ourselves to be accepted as the Principle we were working with. Yet this high thought has always been available to us. Of course there are statements in the textbook which suggest that person is not Principle, but we understand that it was only the indoctrination of orthodox Christian Science that held us to this finite concept.

So, in orthodoxy, we meant God when we referred to Principle. This perpetuated an idea which kept us removed from what is in Truth a fundamental aspect of our divinity. To make you even more aware of this I would like you to accept this now from our textbook:

60. No. 20:11-13

". . . when you eat the divine body of this Principle, [you partake] of the nature, or primal elements, of Truth and Love . . ." [61] That Principle is the fundamental potential which is you. And may I add that there is no need to continue with the words of the following statement for these bring in an element of suffering and martyrdom in connection with this same Principle, understood and practiced. Our higher order of Science rejects this. Go through your concordances and see how many statements there are indicating that Man is Principle. And remember: *that* Man is *you*. Therefore, in our work today, we are not going to study Principle on the one hand as God-infinite and person on the other as finite. We experience here and now the enormous part it plays in our lives and we gratefully identify this living, vital Principle to be us.

How well we know that Principle is often a stand we take consciously, to do, to say, to act, to heal in the highest way we know. Our spiritual authority gives us the strength and power to be Principle; divinely we take charge. Principle is our understanding that the divine Mind is our Mind. Principle is our all-knowing that Soul is forever supreme, expressing itself in numerous ways, satisfying the allness of our being in art, in nature, music and beauty in all its infinite forms. Principle is our sincere feeling that Life, *our* life, is illustrated and defined by our person, and we love the mortal concepts it pictures not only of ourselves but of all our universe ". . . *peopled* with spiritual beings . . ."[62] (italics mine).

Principle is the Truth which gives power to our

61. *S. & H.* 559:24-26
62. *S. & H.* 264:32

language, its clarity and simplicity of expression made demonstrable by conforming to the standards we have set for ourselves. Principle is acceptance of Spirit as our aliveness, and it is participating in the infinite Love that includes the tenderness, strength, spontaneity, enthusiasm and joy that we feel for our entire universe. Yes, Principle includes all; it sums up the God-Principle-Man as our *Present Being*. We read, "For true happiness, man must harmonize with his Principle, divine Love; . . ." [63] and to harmonize with Principle we ". . . unite [identify with] . . . an effect of consonance [agreement]" [64] with our God-Self, divine Love.

Since our work with identity begins with the "I", the first thing is to be in concord with the "I", and by this I mean that each be in concord with himself. In this way we are in harmony with our universe. A hymn says it very well:

> Be true and list the voice within,
> Be true unto thy high ideal,
> Thy perfect self, that knows no sin,
> That self that is the only real.
>
> True to our God whose name is Love,
> We shall fulfill our Father's plan;
> For true means true to God [within],
> To self, and to our fellow-man.[65]

63. *S. & H.* 337:7-8
64. *Webster's New Collegiate Dictionary*—definition of "harmonize."
65. *Christian Science Hymnal*, Page 20

How many times I have heard it said that if only the other fellow were this way or that way, or did this or did that, and the "ifs" go on endlessly. Our work is our own to do. Each one finds his harmony of Being *within himself* by listening to the higher order of Himself. Holding strictly to the harmony of Being is more natural than to have to strive to reach it. It is easier to hold to what you *know* is so, than to have to *try to find* something to believe in.

One year, in looking for a suitable Christmas card, I found one which emphasized the thought of harmony and I was inspired to look up the word in our concordance. As a result I wrote out various references using this word and mailed them with the card because they were so inspirational. If you care to do this yourself you will be surprised to find how many of these references there are! Here are a few of them from *Prose Works*: "Let the reign of peace and harmony be supreme and forever yours." [66] "It is the purpose of divine love to resurrect the understanding, and the kingdom of God, *the reign of harmony already within us.*" [67] "This rule of harmony must be accepted as true relative to man." [68] The definition of heaven, with which I have often asked students to identify, begins with the word "Harmony," and then follows ". . . the reign of Spirit; government by divine Principle; spirituality; bliss; the atmosphere of soul." [69] Understand this to be your experience *now.* Your happiness, your harmony, the Principle of your Being, your heaven is here, pres-

66. *Mis.* 156:11-12
67. *Mis.* 154:16-18 (Italics mine)
68. *Mis.* 187:11-12
69. *S. & H.* 587:25-27

ently, in this very room. It is the atmosphere of Soul!

We understand Principle in such a way that our work as metaphysicians is a joy. There is no need for an advanced student to go through a lot of metaphysical arguing. To be sure, this method had its day and we are grateful for the good we received from it, but it is not needed by us now. We accept realization and we accept Principle as our self-government, our mind-Being, Soul-satisfying, ever-present Life, our constant joy and happiness, our strength, our spiritual sustenance and power. Identifying as Principle takes us into every facet of Life, with all we need to see, hear and know.

All joy remains ours with every happening because we know the principle of Love is in command. We rest in this knowing; we are at peace at all times; we rejoice in the principle of Life as our Being. Put your divine Principle to work in ways you knew not before this day. Accept with me the greatness of this high intent found in our textbook: "God is Love. He is therefore the divine, infinite Principle, called Person or God." [70] This is a statement of the higher order of Person and Principle being *us*. Stay there. Do not go any further with what Mrs. Eddy says in this paragraph, for in it she drops from the high intent and she downgrades the body. We do not accept this concept for ourselves. Our body is a divine idea, the personal likeness of Spirit.

I have a letter in which the writer states "I am reading with a great deal of interest what you say here on page 179, [referring to *The Bridge* [71]], 'We

70. *S. & H.* 302:25-26
71. Irene S. Moore, C.S.: *The Bridge.*

glorified Soul, seeing the wonder and marvel of these bodily elements as divine ideas, the sum total of our own divinity'." Then she states in her letter her own words, ". . . right here on earth in this physical body I have. Apparently, my intuition to see, to be, Soul awareness is in agreement with your words. I have had to acknowledge I have a body — Mind, body, Soul in harmony, right now, right here in this Self existence I am." At the end of her letter she writes, "According to the dictionary 'infinite' means 'Majestic Wholeness'; isn't that great! The majestic wholeness the allness of Mind is, and its manifestation being me, as me and for me. Amen! And it is very good."

In the Association Addresses I have read (and I have read many of them from other Associations than my own), statements from the Bible and from our books are mentioned very often, but references to other books are rarely included. I have wondered about this. Moreover, it is seldom that statements are used which declare a higher order, probably because teachers felt that students were not ready for them, or perhaps that the statements referred to experiences that are impossible to conceive as happening here on earth for a variety of reasons. The quotation I used a moment ago is surely one of these. It is a definition of *your personal person* as infinite Principle even though the word "person" has a capital P in the front of it. Are you ready to accept it for yourself? In the higher order of Self-Identity we do. "God is Love. He is therefore the divine, infinite Principle, called Person or God."

There are three references to person with a capital P in *Science and Health;* there are many more in *Prose Works.* However, you begin to understand why Mrs. Eddy defined God as Person with a capital P when you read in *Miscellany,* page 117:28-32 (italics mine): "I left Boston in the height of prosperity to *retreat* from the *world,* and to seek the one divine Person, whereby and wherein to show others the footsteps from sense to Soul. To give me this opportunity is all that I ask of mankind." The biographies of Mrs. Eddy's life show the long line of difficulties and disappointments she had with persons, so it is understandable that at this time of her life she felt the necessity of turning from person (using lower case lettering) to Person, with capitalization of the first letter, a deified individuality.

In *The Bridge* I wrote a whole chapter to get the idea of person back to a higher order for ourselves. And isn't it glorious that we have Principle back as well!

Here is a letter from a woman who faced the possibility that her foot might be amputated because of gangrene. She called me from the hospital and was most fearful. We rose to the situation, not outlining anything, but rejoicing in Love's omnipresence and omni-action. She finally left the hospital without having to have her foot amputated. This is the letter she wrote to me: "You will be glad to know I have been fitted for walking. Will have to use a cane, but so what? Don't feel I would have made it, without *The Bridge.* Thou art blessed among women. How important to see we are dealing with divine ideas recognizing our divinity *now* —the translation back to MIND."

Take a good look at your life right now, and I mean

all aspects of it. I am sure that all of us rightfully will say, "Yes, Principle governs my life." Principle governs because the God-consciousness which is you is the person of you which is Principle. Think with me for a moment how marvelously ordered and progressive our lives are, how consistently and lovingly drawn to a higher order of our identity. As you read, "Divine Principle is the Life of man," [72] know that *you are* this divine Principle; it is *your* life that is being written about in this passage. Or read, "The infinite Principle [of man] is reflected [expressed] by the infinite idea and spiritual individuality . . ." [73] We are all these ideas in visible, substantial expression.

Go further with your work, knowing that you are the one referred to as you read ". . . that God is divine Love; therefore divine Love is the divine Principle of the divine idea named man; in other words, the spiritual Principle of spiritual man. *Now let us not lose this Science of man, but gain it clearly;* then we shall see that man cannot be separated from his perfect Principle, God, inasmuch as an idea cannot be torn apart from its fundamental basis. This scientific knowledge affords self-evident proof of immortality; proof, also, that the Principle of man cannot produce a less perfect man than it produced in the beginning." [74] As you come upon, "The true idea and Principle of man will then appear,"[75] state it in its present tense; know that it appears for you now, today. As you read, "The perfect man — governed by God, his perfect Principle

72. *S. & H.* 304:17-18
73. *S. & H.* 258:19-20
74. *Mis.* 186:15-24 (Italics mine).
75. *S. & H.* 123:3-4

— is sinless and eternal," [76] this is *you*. There is probably no greater work than this for a student who appreciates the higher order of Science as his personal Identity.

With identification we find that arguments which deprecate self-appreciation disappear. Your God consciousness, Mind, lifts you to grander views and you joyously and freely accept them. I could spend much of this day with the marvelous concepts of man as Principle, but I know, too, what a great and grand discovery is yours as you personally/spiritually and humanly/divinely identify. Do it now with this poem.

RENDERING UNTO CAESAR

XV.

MAN'S word is God in man!
Maintain ye then this living word:
Let it become the vesture of thy soul, thy mantle
without seam,
Also thy clear mirror!
Express thy truth with all thy being's might!
As thou preparest in the secret place, so shall thy
future be!
Accept no circumstance till it become
The fulcrum of the lever of thy truth!
Thou wilt feel the big reality
Meeting thee in all thy ways,
Thy truth as an arrow directed
Speeding to the God-spelt goal on earth;
The hand that draws the bow His word in thee!

76. *S. & H.* 304:14-15

XVI.

THY work may be a continual meditation upon the
   Perfect,
Seeing such therein, working straight thereto!
Thy virtue as a single will to that high end,
   A love, a fire, an energy!
Then daily wilt thou touch Reality,
And feel Love's deep reactions day by day,
   For Life is true to thy truth![77]

I am often asked by students how they may keep the
inspiration of this higher order close to them. To this
I say it is already there as consciousness; they have only
to tune in and hold to it. The higher ideas keep you
inspired, and as you insist on holding to them you gain
a widening view, a tremendous expansion. This in turn
augments the strength to hold to them. Continuing with
the highest we know develops an ability to have this
grand realization always at hand.

The Science of Being, lived by maintaining one's
inspiration, could easily take an entire chapter devoted to the subject of *Practice*. Identity plays a great
part in practice, too.

"HOLY GHOST. Divine Science; the development
of eternal Life, Truth and Love."[78] What, for instance, does this definition mean to you? Well, you understand first of all that "Holy Ghost" means Holy

---

77. *The Cloud and The Fire*, by Robert Whitwell, H. T. Hamblin, Publisher, Bosham, Chichester, England, pages 20, 21. ND
   78. *S. & H.* 588:7-8

Spirit. The word "Holy" means hallowed, as a sanctuary. Sanctuary is a consecrated place. What is more
consecrated than your own God-consciousness? Your
God-consciousness is Spirit. Therefore your Spirit, divine Science, is the Holy Ghost of your own eternal
Life, Truth and Love living you. Reading such definitions and leaving them in the book for the next
reading is not enough; we identify with what we read.
This gives value to our lives and to our work. So, actually, you have a beautiful unfoldment going on as you
apply this triad of Principle.

For the healing of a growth that had been developing in a patient who had called on me for help, I asked
her to work with that definition alone, to know that all
the growth that was going on was the growth (development) of divine Science within her divine Being,
that all there was to her was Life, Truth and Love—
nothing else but this trinity, and that it was demonstrated in her person. Her fear diminished and the
growth disappeared.

———

One day I went to my teacher to tell him that I had
come upon a statement in *Science and Health* that I
felt described the qualifications which were needed for
the practice and teaching of Christian Science. I was
very inspired with it. "THUMMIM. Perfection; the
eternal demand of divine Science. The Urim and
Thummim, which were to be on Aaron's breast when
he went before Jehovah, were holiness and purifica-
tion of thought and deed, which alone can fit us for

the office of spiritual teaching."[79] In the work of translation into the higher order of Science, one purifies his
thought about a great many things by keeping it geared
to Oneness. This brings about the holiness of his deeds.
It secures him to the place of the most high, a location he finds within his own divine Being.

On the other hand our work in orthodox Christian
Science made us aware of two viewpoints of ourselves
and of our universe, and the repetitious work of sense-
testimony denial held priority in our metaphysical work.
On some occasions people send me articles to read
which they have taken from the periodicals in the *hope*
(that I at one time had also) that I may find in them
expressions of Truth based upon the One Mind
premise. Often they are surprised at my reply because
when I send them back I point out the dualistic statements which to me are so conspicuously present. I re-
mind them that the premise of orthodox Christian Science is based on dualism; the Oneness is found only by
our being individually selective, finding it through our
own search for the divine unity that is there all the
time.

It is difficult to get the idea across to a student who
is still conforming to orthodoxy (but desiring to move
on ahead because he sees a little more than he saw before having read *The Bridge*) that as long as he reads
orthodox literature, attends traditional lectures, and
goes to Association Addresses, he will have to read and
hear the dualism because of the premise of orthodox
Christian Science. During my association with the organization several friends sent in articles for publica-

79. *S. & H.* 595:11-16

tion. Their articles were returned for the reason that
they did not present the twoness of thought necessary
to express Christian Science dogma. Corrections were
suggested which were relative to the church viewpoint.
This, of course, is the nature of traditional Christian
Science. The higher order is not yet preferred to the
relative point of view. In other words, the double
premise is preferred. Sometimes my friends changed
their articles to conform and sometimes they did not.
When they were advised to write their articles differently they knew it meant from a premise of "it is"
and "it is not," no matter what the title or the subject matter may have been. I do not mean to say that
such articles are not helpful. I am sure they are for
some, but we let in the higher understanding and stay
with the premise of Oneness.

I am presently working with someone who frequently
sends me articles from the periodicals. One was written
by her teacher, and she wanted to feel that *her teacher*
was stating Christian Science from the Oneness premise that I present in my own works. I understood this
sincere feeling and I remained compassionate because
it was something I went through myself. She wanted
to find in these articles the Oneness she is now appreciating and understanding in her new metaphysical approach. Often we hesitate to give up the old for the
new. I continue to point out to her, however, that the
Oneness, although at times presented in the authorized literature, is not consistently used in the orthodox
teaching. Twoness is emphasized there. I bring this up
because I know that as each one identifies with the
higher order of Himself he recognizes Principle within
demanding Oneness as the nucleus, the radius and

totality of his Science. The whole reason for bringing up this subject at this time is simply to show that you are either identifying with the twoness in your study or you are leaving this work behind you and going on to a higher order of Identity. You alone must make that choice.

Another letter sent to me from one who had just read *The Bridge* states "What wonderful memories your book has brought to me! While we live only in the Now, nevertheless 'All the Good the past has had, remains!'" And she continues, "On page 327 where you write, 'I do not have to be tossed from pillar to post . . .' This is exactly how I used to feel about the periodicals. I would read some very illuminating statement and in the next sentence or paragraph—bang! Down I would come! So confusing, wasn't it? There is so much food for thought in your book it will keep me busy forever! I read and re-read and things constantly unfold—even though I do feel as if I had written it myself!"

A student of Christian Science telephoned me, pointing out a certain passage in *Science and Health* which was challenging the spiritual effort she was making to think the statement through. It had appeared in her Lesson-Sermon for the week. She read it to me and we went on from there. She was giving up the concept of dualism for the divine Oneness in her consciousness and she saw an inconsistency and asked for clarification. Here is the statement she was questioning: "Only impotent error would seek to unite Spirit with matter, good with evil, immortality with mortality, and call this sham unity *man,* as if man were the offspring of both Mind and matter, of both Deity and humanity."[80] Now, of course, her concern was quite understandable because she saw that an agreement with this presentation of Science would be a return to the old dualism she had happily given up. She knew that a synthesis of ideas was what she had been accomplishing in her study of *The Bridge,* namely: the unification of these separates. She was beginning to see that this would never occur within the instruction. With the new view this unification, accepted from a higher order of her Science, would *not* be seen as "impotent error." I pointed out that in challenging the thoughts of this reference we would first have to re-affirm that we accept as a basis that "All is infinite Mind and its infinite manifestation . . ."[81] Then we would be able to translate evil, mortality, and matter into their higher order. In this position we have no erroneous claims.

The higher order of Science acknowledges matter to be as much a part of Mind as Spirit is; our mortality (man) is our immortality (Man) and our humanity is our present divinity. This is the only way to accept "the origin of divinity," the marginal heading, oddly enough, for the very statement we are discussing. Seeing everything now as *potent truth* gives our Science a new look. Then we say, we understand matter/spirit, mortality/immortality, divinity/humanity as potent truth, not as "impotent error." The Oneness in all instances does the work.

I reminded my friend that it is not that error is seeking to unite opposites at all, for to Truth there are no

---

80. *S. & H.* 555:18-22
81. *S. & H.* 468:10-11

opposites. To this she made a marvelous comment and
followed through beautifully. She said: "If I go on
in orthodox Christian Science refusing to see that this
matter universe is divine and refusing to recognize my
mortality as an expression of my immortality, and my
divinity as my humanity, *then in this life there is no
solution for me* because working with metaphysical
arguments in a dualistic system remains a never-end-
ing struggle with this "impotent," illusive error! I think
I'll hold consistently to the statement 'To Truth there
is no error,'[82] or stay with this '. . . Truth that knows
no error . . .'[83] because Truth is what I AM." This is
how she finally resolved her work with this passage.
Her I AM, divine consciousness, kept her thought on
the Oneness, the identity her heart desired.

In *Spirits in Rebellion*,[84] on page 398, we read about
Agnes Sanford. Charles Braden, the author of this
book, states that her language was that of "rational
Christianity." In a story of a man who had no par-
ticular belief about God but who was suffering from
an injury, she recommended this prayer: "Whoever
you are or whatever you are, come into me now and
help nature in my body to mend this bone, and do it
quick. Thanks." We might well ask some important
questions here. Since this man did not believe in God,
he was addressing his prayer to something or to some-

---

82. *No.* 5:7

83. *Mis.* 77:18

84. Charles S. Braden: *Spirits in Rebellion.* Southern Methodist University
Press, Dallas, Texas, 1963.

one other than God—to a power, perhaps one endowed with healing properties. Could we not assume, then, that perhaps he was turning within himself for the healing, addressing what he believed could expand within him to heal? Could it not be his own divinity that he called upon?

On the same page we read another of Mrs. Sanford's experiences. She tells it this way: After slamming a heavy door on a finger, she remarked that "if she had said 'damn' and fought the pain, her finger would have continued to hurt. Instead of this she simply held her finger up and blessed the pain, considering it really as one of God's healing agencies, and then she thought: 'I am a spiritual being . . . My spiritual body has a finger, and that finger doesn't hurt.' A Christian Scientist might well have differed with the idea that she had a spiritual finger . . . The pain ceased at once, she asserts, and quickly the nail resumed its natural color and the incident was forgotten."

At this moment I want to share with you a letter I received recently. My friend is quoting from Kahlil Gibran's book, *The Prophet,* and she found this helpful with a problem she had:

> Your pain is the breaking of the shell
> that encloses your understanding . . .
> And could you keep your heart in wonder
> at the daily miracles of your life, your pain
> would not seem less wondrous than your joy;...

And you would watch with serenity through
the winters of your grief.[85]

This, my friend says, she is doing and with continued
gratitude.

In the higher order of Healing we are grateful for
every expression of healing no matter how or from
where it comes. My interest in this form of expand-
ing universal healing led me to an awareness of what
Kathryn Kuhlman's evangelism was doing. I had read
her two books, *I Believe in Miracles* and *God Can Do
It Again,* so one Sunday morning I decided that I
would attend her meeting at the Shrine Auditorium. I
had been told how crowded it would be and how one
would need a pass to attend, to be seated, but I went
anyhow. The crowd was there alright and as I was
looking around I noticed two nuns standing alone. I
approached and spoke to them. They said they had
come from San Diego with a man from their church.
When I asked for him they said he would be with them
shortly. Soon he arrived. I told him that my husband
and I would like to attend the meeting and if he had
extra passes we would be most grateful to have them.
He gave two of them to me and when we arrived in
the auditorium I was delighted to find we were in the
10th row! It would be difficult to question the healings that took place that day. I must say that my higher
order of Healing (my universal, total acceptance of
God, all-inclusive everywhere) was most grateful for
the experience.

---

85. Kahlil Gibran: *The Prophet.* Random House, New York, 1951, page
52.

I was so impressed that I wrote this letter to Kathryn Kuhlman, February 16th, 1971: "It is a great joy and a privilege to hear and see all the healings that are taking place at the Shrine auditorium through your ministry. Somehow I want you to know that when I read this statement today from one of Mary Baker Eddy's works, 'When the doctrinal barriers between the churches are broken, and the bonds of peace are cemented by spiritual understanding and Love, there will be unity of spirit, and the healing power of Christ will prevail,'[86] I felt that in your own way through the understanding of God you are doing this great work." I also wrote, "My husband is a medical practitioner. He was so impressed by what I told him of the experience a doctor related on your television program that he wrote to this doctor and received a very favorable reply."

Soon after this experience I told a Christian Scientist friend of mine about my going to the Kathryn Kuhlman meeting at the Shrine Auditorium. In telling her what I have written down here I noticed that she neither approved nor criticized me, but later she wrote me a letter expressing the thought that I had not fully understood the article on faith-cure which you can read in *Retrospection and Introspection,* pages 54 and 55. I read it again but did not feel I should cease to be the Love which is grateful for *every* healing I witnessed that day at the Shrine Auditorium, or for that matter for healing anywhere! And I must admit here that for many years I was self-righteous in be-

---

86. *Pul.* 22:16-19

lieving that the only true healing was through Christian Science treatment and that all else was the result of belief instead of understanding, as is suggested by Mrs. Eddy in this article. But I have come a long way since then.

At this time I would like to emphasize some faith-cures in the Bible. After all, for anyone to be healed by faith there would have to be an inner acceptance of identity with wholeness and orderly function and, no doubt, a sincere understanding of God, universal Love. Let us recall the time Jesus said, ". . . thy *faith,* hath made thee whole." We all know the story of the woman who had been diseased for 12 years who ". . . said within herself, If I may but touch his garment, I shall be whole," and who, then, having great *faith,* was healed.

Another story is about the two blind men who asked for mercy. Jesus asked them if they believed that he could heal them. Yes, they believed. "Then touched he their eyes, saying, According to *your faith* be it unto you." (italics mine). Now the woman who was diseased for 12 years must have identified herself with the thought of healing *before* she found herself in the throng around Jesus; and the blind men, no doubt, believed that having sight should be as natural for them as for anyone else. They, too, identified before the healing took place. In *Matthew* 9:26, we read about the man who was sick of the palsy, lying on a bed. He was brought to Jesus by some people who believed that Jesus could heal him. ". . . and Jesus *seeing their faith* [italics mine] said unto the sick of the palsy; Son, be of good cheer, thy sins be forgiven thee . . . Arise, take up thy bed and go unto thine house." This same faith enabled many of the prophets to do wondrous things *because they believed*. (Read chapter 11 of *Hebrews*. From start to finish it is a chapter on the greatness of faith). I also want to add here that in our understanding we accept the following concept of believing taken from the *Glossary*: "BELIEVING. Firmness and constancy; . . . the perception of spiritual Truth." (*S. & H.*, page 582:1-2)

In the higher order of Healing we are grateful for every comfort given to man from anyone and from any place. We are thankful for all the wondrous performances in whatever aspect they appear. We do not limit the power of God, of goodness; we continue to rejoice at the ever-widening appearances of the universality of healing coming to man from so many infinite sources. This is, in fact, the infinity of our own God-conscious identity recognizing the allness of Love.

Orthodox Christian Scientists (and I was one) are indoctrinated with the thought that *only* Christian Science heals and that all other healings are merely faith-cures. By this is meant they do not have the sanction of the Truth and thus are not worth entertaining in consciousness. However, one can reason with his God-consciousness and be healed of this self-righteousness. My own gratitude remains steadfast regardless of the manner in which a healing is obtained.

When a dear friend of mine in New York City (not a Christian Scientist) wrote to me about his happy experience with acupuncture, I knew I would remain consistent with my premise that "All is infinite Mind and its infinite manifestation, for God is All-in-all," and I praised and glorified God, Good, for this person's healing. He wrote: "I had heard from a friend of mine that a Chinese woman doctor was giving treatments in downtown Chinatown. Getting the address I went there twice for acupuncture treatment from her. I reported arthritis as the trouble, and I told her I was in pain constantly. I had two treatments and 'lost it.' It was quite an experience. I've forgotten about my arthritis as though it never happened."

My friend has been dedicated to metaphysics through the years and has been as sincere in his own religious understanding as a Christian Scientist is to his. He simply went about identifying with his wholeness; he did not outline insistently how his healing was to occur. Knowing him as I do, I am sure that his spiritual integrity, his faith in his own divine goodness, made him whole. We should not let our ignorance of something permit prejudiced barriers to set up limitations for ourselves or for our universe. In the higher order of Knowledge the divine Mind pierces this ignorance and permits our mind, the divine Mind, to be governed and directed individually according to the law of healing and love. Neither can we reject the continued probing of Man's mind into more expansive areas where he may explore other fields that sustain and maintain life.

Some of you may have recently read a story which appeared in *The Los Angeles Times* concerning the parents who through "faith" and a strong belief in collective prayer took insulin away from their child in a decision of confidence that the Lord had healed him. The child died, but the parents went even further. They believed through prayer and God's love that their child would rise from the dead in three days and would prove how unshakable had been their faith. This did not happen either. Right here I wish to say that I would have glorified their faith had the healing taken place, as they prayed it might, even if it could be called faith-cure. I would have rejoiced with them no matter what their beliefs if their prayer had been answered for them.

Here you might well ask what has all this got to do with Identity. I clearly and emphatically state that the God-consciousness Love exists everywhere for everyone no matter what the label is—in the evangelists who are establishing their ministries of healing by the Holy Spirit, in the psychologists who are probing behavior patterns, in the analysts who are delving into the human mind, in the Christian Scientists who heal through spiritual understanding, and in the acupuncture specialists or anyone else who works for healing with sincerity and love. All are part of the healing identity. They are promoting the wholeness of Man as he was in the beginning and ever shall be: purposeful, fulfilled, satisfied, resourceful and productive in extending the love of God, Good, as an identity in the health and harmony of Man, Present Being.

We are not practicing universal love in our approach to healing unless we include *all,* and identify with the allness which is God. To do otherwise is to limit the omnipotence, omnipresence, omni-action and omniscience of God, Good.

In concluding this higher order of Healing Identity and its universal Allness, I want to tell a story of a woman I went to see one morning who had been in pain during the night. Not only was she in physical pain when I saw her, but she wanted in some way to be exonerated for something she had done during the previous night. Although she hesitated to tell me about it, she finally did, and here is what she said. She had been told by a friend about a telephone number she could dial at any time in order to receive a healing message. With apologies, she admitted she had done this. The healing message comforted her very much; in fact, she said, it sounded in some ways like a Christian Science treatment, although she knew it was in truth a point of view spoken by a member of the Religious Science Church. When she told me what was said I recognized it to be a message on the Allness of God, and I told her so.

Shortly after this a Christian Science nurse arrived who had been on the case for a few days. Upon hearing the same story, she became very disturbed. She said she did not think she could remain on the case because she felt that if a patient read anything or listened to anything but Christian Science the healing would be retarded. She then told us that her teacher warned her students that only harm could come from mixing any other healing methods with Christian Science because all other healing methods were false teaching—and then she hurriedly left us. Of course we did not agree with the stand she took, but at the same time we understood that she was practicing the highest she knew and we blessed her for her integrity. We went on being grateful for ever-present Love in whatever form it presented itself to us and we were inspired with Truth as it unfolded. Before long the patient was completely free from her pain through a knowledge of her spiritual identity and we went on rejoicing.

This is a good illustration of the rigid attitude toward healing that the instruction of Christian Science introduces. We take a higher view than this by seeing the goodness wherever it may be. To be comforted by a healing message from whatever source is receiving wholeness of a kind, and this cannot be limited to a sect or to any special group. A friend of mine had something very good to say about this. She writes that Christian Science members are taught the "conviction that Christian Science is the only correct method of healing." And she goes on to say "this very Science . . . *seen in all its universal and infinite glory will remove that restriction.*" (italics mine). How true this is and how wonderful to contemplate the glory of the higher order that is universal and infinitely glorious.

On September 16, 1972, I received this letter from a student who was overjoyed in working with the wonderful statements she was finding which were helping her to maintain a consistent joy as the Science of Being. She states: "I *had* to have some *real* Science or my interest would have been completely disillusioned . . . it seemed that everything I studied became a mental 'foot-ball' between the two concepts. For [a great many] years it did not change although I knew within that there would have to be a balance somewhere. This started when I worked with the Cern lecture that I mentioned . . . the statement 'All is infinite Mind'— and he added 'instead.' Until your book appeared I was satisfied in my thinking that I could stand on that statement. So, since then it has begun to 'burst out all over.' In *The Bridge,* page 363, the last five lines, I quote ' "Of two things fate cannot rob us: namely, of choosing the best, and of helping others to choose." [*My*. 165:2-3]. If one wishes, he may use both Christian Science and medical science, or either one, and still have *faith* in the One Mind. In either case he is "choosing the best," and Love does the work.' "

Later she wrote me again, referring to pages 364 and 365 in my book. She says, "[the following] completes the thought that explains my remarks in my last letter. If there is any choice at all choose 'The Higher Order' rather than . . . the comparative, competitive and contradicting concepts of the dualistic approach. 'Perfection is gained only by perfection.' Now we start practicing from this point of view instead . . . of arguing and tossing the belief around until it is worn out and finally gives up!" What she means is that *we identify as Perfection* from the very beginning.

All of this simply shows how a higher order of Identity develops within us from our early understanding of Christian Science as we progress to see the wholeness of our Being. Then it happens that we get into the realization immediately without the laborious work of denial and affirmation. Every advanced student is ready for this metaphysical approach; as a matter of fact, his scientific work lovingly directs him to it. In traditional Christian Science instruction one becomes so involved in the sin, sickness and death concepts that he has to labor a great deal with these claims because the claims themselves become very real. Then it is difficult for him to see every healing as an expression of Mind no matter what his surroundings may be. Students of orthodoxy tend to work too hard with its relative aspects and work too little with the perfection now.

Their healing successes might well be more numerous with the higher viewpoint. *Our joy remains with us* as we look out from the heights instead of allowing our thought to pry deep down into erroneous causes. But remember: we do not interfere with the one who is still needing the preliminary work in the instruction. We permit him his stage of identity, for wherever he may be he is in his highest understanding of good.

I would like to tell another story about a guest in my home who was making an afghan. It had a beautiful star-shell design as its pattern. As she progressed she noticed that the upper half of the shell did not fit evenly with the half star-shell below, and when she measured the afghan, after many rows of crocheting, she noticed that it was much looser than it should have been, although the number of patterns across was correct. She was spending a great deal of time finding out what the error was without arriving at a solution. I knew somehow we had to turn our thought to the perfect stitch. I suggested that she write to the yarnshop and ask them to send her the perfect pattern in the mail. Shortly after this they sent her one and, having the perfect model before her, the beautiful design took on its perfect pattern.

The reason that I am sharing this with you is that she and I had been having a conversation regarding the meaning of a statement by Mrs. Eddy. My guest felt that perhaps the premise of Allness which I presented in *The Bridge* might be somewhat too absolute for members to accept — that there were occasions when one *had* to consider mortal mind, animal magnetism and erroneous, universal influences and beliefs. To support this point of view she very properly quoted a statement with which we all are familiar: "A knowledge of error and of its operations must precede that understanding of Truth which destroys error . . ."[87] This statement used to keep us very busy trying to find out all about the error which had to be eradicated. Remember how we were supposed to probe deeply into mortal mind, to analyze our thinking and attitudes? In fact we had to do just about everything we could to get to the bottom of the error!

On the other hand, there is another of Mrs. Eddy's statements which says simply and beautifully, that "Perfection is gained only by perfection."[88] In these differing ideas one can make a choice as to his metaphysical work, but *in the higher order of Science* we emphasize the latter one exclusively. This is the identification that springs from the premise of Oneness, the Allness of God.

One sees how far he has advanced in Christian Science by the statements he upholds and voices as his Science. Should he choose the first reference, in which he is instructed to learn about error to destroy it, there is a strong indication that the concept of error still holds an important place in his consciousness. His continuing work with Truth helps him to "unsee" the error by replacing it with a higher understanding and this "higher understanding" means seeing the perfection of what appeared as imperfection. Then it follows that we ask why we should have to replace something with Truth when that something is already Truth. Remember our premise that "All is infinite Mind and its infinite manifestation." Choose the second state-

87. *S. & H.* 252:8-10
88. *S. & H.* 290:19-20

ment for your spiritual enlightenment. Accept a higher order of Interpretation for your present understanding. This is your identity—that to which you choose to give your loyalty.

———————

I received this letter from a couple who were in my Association when I was a member of the Christian Science church. She says, "I decided that not another day would go without my answering your dear letter. [Incidentally] my husband informs me that there is no one to write to and no one to do the writing. Would you believe???" Well, as I went on with her letter it was quite clear that *this* wife was not in the annihilating business, but her husband was seeing his world as vacuous with no person, place or thing, and he was busily employed with the relative aspects of the instruction of Christian Science where nothing is tangibly real and where all the material world is an illusion *including his wife who was writing the letter to me!* In the last line he must have made a kind of compromise, however, for she says: "Bill joins in sending to you both dearest love." You see, he had to admit that we do exist after all! We *are* persons and we *do* live in the reality of Being here and now!

I should also like to tell you about a friend who was having a problem with someone whose name is Benjamin. She is a very consecrated, orthodox Christian Scientist and in her concern she studied the definition of *Benjamin* in the *Glossary*. She was interpreting her friend within the context of the first part of the definition, the one which describes all the faults attributed to Benjamin. She felt that *her* Benjamin had all these faults also and that this was the reason why she was having all the trouble. Here is the first part of the definition she was reading and identifying as her friend:

> BENJAMIN . . . A physical belief as to life, substance, and mind; human knowledge, or so-called mortal mind, devoted to matter; pride; envy; fame; illusion; a false belief; error masquerading as the possessor of life, strength, animation, and power to act.[89]

Certainly with this as her definition (identity) it looked as though she had a very bad case of Benjamin on her hands! I asked her if she had spent any time with the second part of the definition which I knew contained a higher concept. She said she had not. We turned to it and went over it in detail. Soon she began to have a different image of Benjamin.

Let us remember always that both definitions are part of Mind—but we have a choice. Just because a definition is part of Mind does not mean that we have to accept it. All the statements about Benjamin in the first part of the definition (a description of a mortal as though he had no spirituality at all) were, no doubt, factors which led this friend of mine to see *her* Benjamin as a state of mortal mind and error. The second part (which turned her completely around about him) is this:

> . . . Renewal of affections, self-offering; an improved state of mortal mind; the introduc-

---

89. *S. & H.* 582:4-8

tion of a more spiritual origin; a gleam of the infinite idea of the infinite Principle; a spiritual type; that which comforts, consoles, and supports.[90]

With a change of emphasis and acceptance of a higher order of Benjamin, her harmony was restored. Do we in this class-room today have Josephs, Roberts, Marys, Alices, Richards etc. needing to be translated? Let's do it now! We cannot afford to indulge ourselves in all the claims of what is referred to by some as error, to get caught up in them, to become unnecessarily involved, wondering why this happened or has not happened. We keep our minds filled with Life, Truth and Love and we go on to further enlightenment in reaching beyond "an improved state of mortal mind," an introduction or just a gleam. Our present work is to behold all as the perfect image regardless of situation or condition. We *see* perfection; we keep our peace and just *love*.

Every story I have told in this class is one of identification. I have another one about a man who had just returned from the hospital where he had been given some blood tests. He was home when he called me and his concern was about what these tests might reveal. He was fearful that they would report something that would be considered serious. I told him that he had a choice in his approach to what concerned him: he could panic, or he could know the presence of his God-consciousness, bringing him a grand sense of se-

90. *S. & H.* 582:9-13

renity and assurance that *all is well,* and he could see substance, body, as being all good, all God. He could hold to a higher order of Substance for his experience, and bring to his situation a quiet confidence, and assurance that Love is present as his being all the way. I gave him the wonderful statement from *Isaiah* 30:15, ". . . in quietness and in confidence shall be thy strength: . . ." and it was. Knowing our God-consciousness reigns is putting our minds at rest; it is letting our Christ-consciousness, which is ever-present and available to us, be our steadfast support. This is the harmony of our Being that is always at hand.

In *The Bridge,* page 299, we read: "As a practitioner, it has been a great liberation to stay poised as Mind in all situations. The orthodox Christian Scientist is often beside himself making what he calls his demonstration. When he does not objectify what he has outlined he feels he has failed. Then, overcome by the failure, he cannot see that whatever is taking place for him *is* the demonstration!" Now to return to the man who was worrying about his blood tests. He received the assurance he needed, for shortly thereafter I received this letter: "I was released from the hospital. My stay in the hospital was absolutely without fear, regret or guilt of any kind. It seemed as though I had to go through this experience again. It was really a happy experience. Your book helped to release me from the belief that I had reached a point in my life where nothing could help me, not even Christian Science. My thought has been lifted to a higher level. [Now] I can see and understand that 'God is all,' absolutely that." A few days later I received another letter from this same person. "I neglected to tell you that the arthritis I mentioned to you the first time I called about a month ago has practically cleared up. I am sure this is due to the fact that I have finally cleared out of my thinking the orthodox belief of any other power except God's law of eternal *good*."

Yes, we must look at what is going on and rejoice in the knowledge that *whatever the appearance,* it is Mind being manifest for our ultimate good. I have told patients to stop outlining and "be surprised." Then there is no fear, no anxiety. They relax in their divinity, acknowledging the forever God, good, as their Being and experiencing a peace that requires no outlining. Mrs. Eddy says, "All reality is in God and His Creation . . ."[91] In the higher order of our Science this reality is God being you and your creation. This is present reality for you, so it is natural to love what you are and what your experience is, seeing it all as good.

Joseph must have had a remarkable awareness of his spirituality. Long before his brothers had conspired to put him in a pit out of their sight, he had dreamed dreams of what he knew to be his identity. And he told them so. He would live to save them. He knew his power, his strength and saving grace not only for them but for a nation.

In this remarkable story, Joseph was taken out of the pit and brought ". . . down to Egypt; and [a] . . . captain of the guard, an Egyptian, bought him of the hands of the Ishmeelites . . ."[92] His dreams which had

91. *S. & H.* 472:24
92. *Genesis* 39:1

so disturbed his brethren, because he saw them as servants and he as their Lord, were to come to pass. Pharaoh was looking for someone to interpret his own dreams and his servants told him of Joseph. With the interpretation Joseph gave him of the seven lean years and seven fruitful years, he made plain the work to be done for the saving of Egypt from famine. Joseph's awareness of his God-consciousness led him to say to his brothers, when they were disturbed at having placed him in the pit, "So now *it was not you* that sent me hither, *but God*: and he hath made me a father to Pharaoh, and lord of all his house . . ."[93] And later he was able to say to them also, "Fear not: for *am I* in the place of God? But as for you, ye thought evil against me; *but God meant it unto Good,* to bring to pass, as it is this day, *to save much people alive.*"[94]

As long as we identify as God, Good, nothing in our experience can be turned to evil, nothing that has ever been done to us will have been evil. No condition or circumstance could be evil because to the Truth which we are *there is no evil.* All is God, good.

When Mrs. Eddy states that Principle and its idea, man, are coexistent and eternal, she is referring to somebody that does not exist before our eyes because in the traditional view one is too mortal to attain to such a lofty ideal *in the flesh.* But you accept this today as applying to *your* character, *your* constitution, *your* nature, *your* individuality, the man that you have accepted yourself to be, and you rejoice in the eternality of it as your Mind-identity.

Should you read the statement, "Become conscious

---

93. *Genesis* 45:8 (Italics mine)
94. *Genesis* 50:19-20 (Italics mine)

for a single moment that Life and intelligence are purely spiritual,—neither in nor of matter,—and the body will then utter no complaints,"[95] you realize at once that you must eliminate the phrase "neither in nor of matter" to make this sentence one of the Higher Order. Why? Because we do not deny matter concepts. We accept them as manifestations of Spirit. Life and intelligence are *in* matter because "All is infinite Mind and its infinite manifestation . . ." With this as our premise it cannot be otherwise.

All is spirit/matter Mind and its infinite manifestation. In a metaphysical treatment we do not change our bodies *from* matter *to* Spirit; we accept them as having present existence in *perfect present* harmony (Spirit) and we expect them to demonstrate what in Truth they already are. We are not getting rid of anything, certainly not matter; we are recognizing its spirituality right here, right now. And does not the demonstration take place in the physical form? This is the evidence of Truth's work. Be grateful for all matter concepts; they include everything we behold as well as all the marvelous services they give us. I have pointed out this new view of matter many times in my practice of Christian Science and it is emphasized in my book.

Someone who had been studying *The Bridge* and was appreciating its premise once said to me that if she accepted the higher order of Science as I have been presenting it there would be nothing left for her to do. When I asked her to explain it further, she said there would be no denying of evil, no "work" as she had

---

95. *S. & H.* 14:12-15
96. *S. & H.* 520:3-5

known it in orthodoxy. About that kind of "work" I readily agreed with her, but I also assured her that her *real* work was just beginning as the *realization of what is*. What a joy it is to step into the higher order of God as one's Being and identify *as it* all the time! And I mean in a hospital, in a pit, or wherever you are. Her "work" now is identification: realizing the One Mind, accepting for herself the all-inclusiveness of Love: "The depth, breadth, height, might, majesty, and glory of infinite love [that] fill all space."[96] And to this Mrs. Eddy adds: "That is enough!" We hold enthusiastically to this as our identity and we delete the thoughts in the paragraph that follow, for instance, that "The absolute ideal, man, is no more seen nor comprehended by mortals, than is his infinite Principle, Love."[97] This "absolute ideal, man" *is* identified, seen and comprehended by you as *your* infinite Principle. If this is not so, then where is this absolute, ideal man to be found? Our new work is appreciating this higher order of Man as ourselves in the flesh, right here in our mortality, our corporeality, our person.

So, actually, in the new work we have a happy time accepting for our identity many thoughts we once felt we might never apply to our present lives. And we learn that all the wonderful ideas about ourselves need not be postponed until we are so ethereal that we no longer have a body or a universe.

You may appreciate a letter written by a young lady. She says, "Mom recommended that I start with the chapter on *Person* [this is referring to *The Bridge*]. I

97. *S. & H.* 520:7-9

never could fully understand the dualistic approach to man that I was taught in the Sunday School. Your approach is so feasible and refreshing. Also I enjoy the examples you use to illustrate your ideas." And then she asks this question. "I wish you could explain something to me when you write back. I recognize that man is a single entity without two selves, spiritual and material. Isn't using the words 'human footsteps' nullifying this, or is it just that man can't sit back and not do what he is supposed to do?" I was happy that she brought this up, and when I answered her letter I told her that she was absolutely correct. The term "human footsteps" to the traditional Christian Scientist did not make him feel very good, for it meant something earthly, physical, a material activity that had to be tolerated, to be put up with, until such time as he did not have to experience it anymore. Yet, every orthodox student knows he cannot sit in a corner doing nothing and expect something to happen. He finally has to take the "human footsteps" after all, so he has to compromise situations and this does not bring him the fullness of joy he should have. However, in the higher order of Science we learn that those human footsteps are the divine, so we have no dualism to disturb us whatsoever. We go further knowing we are cause, causation, direction, fulfillment—and every step is a step divine.

There is no division of activity as to what is human and what is divine. They are One. With this understanding we bring a more personal awareness of our Science into concrete form so that we realize better the full potential of our living, acting, all-seeing, all-knowing, exuberant Science. *It is our identity* and we

happily utilize it in all circumstances that come to us.
You know the hymn on page 66 of our hymnal; let
me recall the words for you:

> O perfect Mind, reveal Thy likeness true,
> That higher selfhood which we all must prove,
> Joy and dominion, love reflecting [expressing]
> Love. Alleluia! Alleluia!

Let us rejoice that we are doing it with all the
humanness as well as divineness which is our divinity.
Take one more look at the word *human;* in it you find
the word *man.* Now take your *Glossary* and study in
such a way that you are presently identified as Man.
(*S. & H.* 591:5-7).

As one continues to let his identity reveal itself there
is plenty to do—but with joy and dominion. We appreciate our new selectivity; our horizons broaden; we
ponder statements we may not have seen before. We
no longer hesitate to be our own authority in translations we used to take for granted, or which we puzzled
over but would not question their validity, the contradictions they presented, or their relativeness. We feel
free now to challenge these if we wish and in ways that
are new to us! We actually identify with those thoughts
we once considered too absolute! In the higher order
of our Glorified Humanness we appreciate who we are
and what we are.

Reading *Science and Health* we may come to a
paragraph on page 380 under the marginal heading
A higher discovery. In this reference is the following:
"Many years ago the author made a spiritual discovery,
the scientific evidence of which has accumulated to

prove that the divine Mind produces in man health, harmony, and immortality." *Accept this discovery for yourself today.* To us, here, now, it is *our* divine Mind that is this very discovery, producing in *us* health, harmony and immortality, and therefore we identify as it. We augment this very Mind in us from the substance of ourselves, seeing Godliness in all, the consciousness of health and harmony everywhere.

Since the subject of this class is titled *Identity,* I want to suggest some thoughts I have given women who feel that many of their ailments come from just being women: that is, females, mothers, or brides. The allegory of Adam and Eve and the terrible curse said to have been placed on her are used to explain many of women's troubles. On top of this is the guilt that accompanies the sensual joys we are taught to annihilate, or at least to sublimate, in *orthodox Christian Science.* There are many references in our textbook to substantiate this; for example: "The sinless joy,—the perfect harmony and immortality of Life, possessing unlimited divine beauty and goodness *without a single bodily pleasure or pain,*—constitutes the only veritable, indestructible man, whose being is spiritual."[98] Our orthodox work in general was to annihilate the five physical senses and we know that many of our Lesson-Sermons perpetuated these ideas also.

I ask women to identify with acceptance of a higher concept of themselves as Woman. "BRIDE. Purity and innocence, conceiving man in the idea of God; a

---

98. *S. & H.* 76:22-26 (Italics mine)

sense of Soul, which has spiritual bliss and enjoys but cannot suffer."[99] There are many more. In *Revelation* 12:16 we read "And the earth helped the woman . . ." and in *Science and Health* 517:10, "The ideal woman corresponds to Life and to Love." Unless you identify with what you are reading, the words are meaningless. I suggest that women read an article titled *One Point of View—The New Woman* from *Pulpit and Press*[100] and identify with all the wonderful concepts so beautifully enumerated in it. Here we recognize the genius of Mrs. Eddy shining through many of her statements about woman and womanhood. I leave this work for you to expand upon. Go into it in a joyous, wonderful way and *identify* with your womanliness.

Before leaving this subject, let me give you another reference from our books:

> To-day there are ten thousand Esthers, and Miriams by the million, who sing best by singing most for their own sex. They are demanding the right to help make the laws, or at least to help enforce the laws upon which depends the welfare of their husbands, their children and themselves. . . . With the assurance of faith she prays, with the certainty of inspiration she works, and with the patience of genius she waits. At last she is becoming 'as fair as the morn, as bright as the sun' . . .'[101]

These pertinent and timely thoughts were writ-

---

99. *S. & H.* 582:14-16
100. *Pul.* pp. 81 through 84
101. *Pul.* 82:22-27 and 83:10-13

ten in *The New Century,* February, 1895. They are
beautiful for woman's liberated identity today. We
cannot possibly limit their essential value to Mrs.
Eddy's time for they ring just as true for our present-
day women. *This* is the time for *The New Woman,*
now, in this century, and you are this woman. Take
your concordances and look up everything on women,
woman, womanhood, remembering always to be selective in order to identify with the highest concept of
your true womanhood. "This is woman's hour, with
all its sweet amenities and its moral and religious reforms."[102] Have you ever read this: "To one 'born
of the flesh,' however, divine Science must be a discovery. *Woman must give it birth.*"[103] I identified
with this following thought and from it I brought
forth *The Bridge.* "And woman, the spiritual idea,
takes of the things of God and showeth them unto
the creature, until *the whole sense of being is leavened
with Spirit.*"[104] The "whole sense of being" includes
all that we know in our experiences no matter what
form it may take. "All is infinite Mind and its infinite manifestation . . ."

———

Not long ago, I was talking on the telephone with
a friend who wished to share a passage with me from
Nora Holmes' *The Runner's Bible.* She quoted the
following: "Never think of your spiritual body as
having the form of your physical body because eyes

102. *No.* 45:19-20
103. *Ret.* 26:22-23 (Italics mine).
104. *Mis.* 175:2-5 (Italics mine).

see only in one direction and arms reach only so far."
To me, of course, this sounded just like the dualism,
with its ideas of limitation, that I left behind. When
I asked her to describe this spiritual body without its
physical form she could not. Her answer was so indefi-
nite and vague that we both had a good laugh! If anyone in this class today can show us his spiritual body
without his physical form please do so that we may see
it!

When I first started to study Christian Science I
used to have a metaphysical game with myself. I
wanted so much to see and know more about this
spiritual body that I would stand in front of a mirror
and close my eyes so that my physical body would not
be evident to me. I waited and waited, wondering if
evidence of something would be revealed which I
could identify differently from what I saw as physique.
I suppose that in a way I was looking for an integra-
tion of physicality and spirituality even at that early
time in my life. It was a fragmentary suggestion of
what has since become my conviction.

My thoughts on the higher order of Christian Science did not begin with my writing of *The Bridge*.
They started back in 1943 during World War II. In
a letter to my husband I told him that I had been
picking grapes and when I came home I found my
arms covered with poison ivy. This is what I wrote:
"But, it isn't anything to be alarmed about, and it will
pass I am sure. It is strange that I have no fear of
poison ivy. *I do not protect myself against it* the way I
might have a year ago [with relative Christian Science thinking] and there is no reason for me to have
it at all. But it is an indication that I believe in mat-

ter and that there are two substances: matter to give off something (erroneous?—the ivy) and matter which can take it on—me. So I have decided to come up higher and know there is only One Mind, One Power and that that Power is good. It is an opportunity for me right now to know there is no adversity in Mind." Even then my Science was making itself known to me in a higher form than before. This was in its early beginning, and I am happy to share it with you in this class.

Interestingly enough, in this same letter I was quoting some ideas from *The Unobstructed Universe,* by Stewart Edward White, and I mentioned that I had not yet found *The Betty Book.* Someday, I would like to write a book of the letters written to my husband when he was overseas during World War II. They indicate how steeped I was in the orthodox instruction. My obedience to the letter of Christian Science and my earnestness and devotion to its higher ideals shows very clearly in them. Traditional Christian Science was my main interest during his early military service but these letters reveal the direction toward Oneness I was taking. Some years after his return I became a Christian Science practitioner.

Perhaps this is the place for me to tell this class that I never entertained any idea of resigning from the Christian Science organization. Why should I? I found everything *in its highest teaching* that my heart, soul and mind desired, and I have always been grateful for the part it played in my life, for the steady growth it provided me on my way to accepting a higher Science as my being.

My desire was to remain in the organization, to go

on teaching the higher order I found within its doctrine, but I now find my desire is being fulfilled in ways I could never have outlined, and I rejoice. In my practice I recognized the need of healing but I was also teaching the divine allness. To my patients I introduced the higher order of Science showing them how to integrate ideas on the premise of Oneness, and I emphasized the fact that we have a *choice* in our work as Christian Scientists. With the publication of *The Bridge,* however, both my branch church and *The Mother Church* felt I was no longer the orthodox student I had been and, of course, they were correct. I had taken Mrs. Eddy's works and to my spiritual satisfaction and joy found within them a higher order of Science. For interpreting from my divine withinness, for promoting this higher order within Christian Science and for showing, in some instances, the necessity to up-date the Science of Being in a more practical and identifiable way, I was excommunicated from the organization.

The situation I found myself in and the reaction of The Board of Directors of *The Mother Church* are very much like those appearing in a cartoon I saw in *The New Yorker Magazine,* 1972, done by Sauers. It shows a very happy man walking along the street, apparently a demonstrator. He is carrying a sign on which is written, "ITS A GREAT BIG WONDERFUL WORLD THAT WE LIVE IN!" Near him is a policeman looking somewhat surprised. He is listening to a man on the sidewalk who is pointing to the demonstrator and shouting "Officer, arrest that man!"

———

In the January/February, 1972, *Laird Letter,* Margaret Laird states:

> A comment from 'official Boston' speaks of Mrs. Moore as considering herself to be voicing 'a higher order of Science.' So true, and so badly needed today when the Christian Science organization is apparently sinking to the level of a Christian denominational religion . . . This fact of Science as individual conscious identity, one's self, is 'the higher order of Science,' the pure metaphysics of Spirit. In the vision that is from and as Science, there is no end to the new worlds unfolding from within and as one's self. The semi-metaphysics of Christian theology divides consciousness into Mind and matter, Spirit and flesh, subject and object, and from this illusory dualism stems our wants and woes. Mrs. Eddy addresses those who are *called* to voice a 'Higher Order of Science'; 'Obey this call . . . take not back the words of Truth.' (*Misc. Writ.* 99:12-15).
>
> Mrs. Moore's book and my own books are based, not only on the Science of Christian Science as stated variously by Mrs. Eddy, but are written from our practice of this Science . . . In this living, the personal concept no longer hides the divine individuality . . . Mrs. Moore's book is autobiographical in the sense that it presents the self-fulfilling God-idea or Science, as it evolves from within and as herself. *The Bridge* might be called the evolution

of consciousness, 'the extra-terrestrial life' (heaven on earth) that demonstrates absolute Christian Science here and now . . . The new language of 'the higher order of Science' does not reject the old as wrong, but as inadequate for today. This is the day of Science demonstrating the co-existence of the human and divine. No division of consciousness into human and divine!

From letters I am receiving since having written *The Bridge,* I notice that students are drawn quite naturally to the higher order of their Being almost without knowing how it happened. It seems to be proper direction for their lives giving free reign to its natural and divine unfoldment. Sooner or later in the orthodox church they learn that if they question anything in Christian Science which might be unfolding to them they would often be chided for having doubted. Many consecrated, dedicated Christian Scientists feel they are being disloyal if they challenge *any* statement in their books. They have been indoctrinated with the idea that these writings have a divine authorization. Actually what really has taken place in many of them is the realization that they could no longer identify with many statements they were reading. They had outgrown them and were holding to what they believed to be more advanced statements. So, we see that identity was playing its important part all along the way.

In the book entitled *Christian Science & Liberty,*[105]

---

105. Robert E. Merritt and Arthur Corey: *Christian Science & Liberty.* DeVorss & Company, Santa Monica, California, 1970, page 47.

by Robert E. Merritt and Arthur Corey, one finds frank disclosures of their experiences in quoting from unauthorized literature and the results which followed. Mr. Merritt's honest evaluation of himself in his liberation from orthodoxy is just another example of what happens to one who is seeking the Science of Being within his own divine being. He states his experience this way: "I found that my resignation was not prompted by either fear or resentment; paradoxically, I had come to have a strange new sense of liberty and cleanliness, a closeness to God that was peaceful and reassuring . . ."

As we identify with liberty and with freedom of conscience, we joyously explore every avenue of Christian Science. Let me state right here that *you are* the authorized word of God and all of your questionings are the operation of your divine intelligence, your own independent, free-evolving quality of your Godliness. Questioning anything is Love seeking its own divine explanation; it is Mind (your mind) magnificently elaborating itself!

Now how do we fulfill the meaning of these thoughts without the premise of Oneness to work with? It is a necessity for us to question and wonder if we are to identify as the Truth; this is why we translate writings. It is the power of Truth within us exemplifying a higher formulation of our identity. We all know the statement: "Ye shall know the Truth and the Truth shall make you free." In the traditional instruction we studied in order to know *about* the Truth that was going to make us free sometime later. In the higher order of Identity we *are* the Truth itself and this knowledge frees us now to be our own authority. The premise of Oneness is required to permit us this freedom.

One of the reasons we have such a high regard for Jesus is that he felt free to dispute the authority of the elders. Not only did he challenge many of the concepts in the Old Testament but he expanded upon them. Read *Matthew* 5, beginning with verse 21 through 48. Pay attention to statements such as these: "Ye have heard that it was said . . ." and "But I say unto you . . ." and then note the change Jesus is making regarding these scriptural statements. In other words he is contesting the beliefs of the scribes and Pharisees of his day; his ideas are based upon a different premise.

We know also, according to the law of the Old Testament, that the Jews had no dealings with the Samaritans, but Jesus pays no attention to this law, for he spent time in Samaria with the woman at the well teaching her the true nature of worship, introducing himself as the Messiah, saying, "I that speak unto thee am he." (John 4:26). This statement of Identity spoken with authority, and his willingness to talk with the woman of Samaria to proclaim his zeal for God's glory, broke down the long standing barrier which existed between the Jews and the Samaritans. He changed the law by expressing his loving identity to a Samaritan woman.

Once I asked a patient, who said she was feeling quite depressed, to stop everything and sit down and read all the testimonies in the chapter on *Fruitage* in *Science and Health*. I was surprised and delighted at her frank, unhesitant honesty with me. She said, "Oh,

Mrs. Moore, don't ask me to do that. It would make me *more miserable*." When I inquired into her reasoning I realized that I was about to learn something from her. She said she did not want to be reminded of all the diseases mentioned in the many testimonies that were there. She told me that she had read them for more than forty years, and she practically knew them by heart. She said she appreciated them when she was an early student in Christian Science but after these many years she simply could not do it anymore. I did not know then (but I do now) that her mind, the divine mind, ever-present even in the midst of her misery, was now directing her away from going over again all the illnesses described in *Fruitage* even though the testimonies at the same time voiced healings that came to many from simply having read the Christian Science textbook.

She preferred a new identity for herself, and I thanked her for not hesitating to tell me so. We started our metaphysical work by glorifying our present divinity, by holding to thoughts of health, harmony and peace, and by simply knowing "God's law is in three words, 'I am ALL' . . ."[106] I saw the divinity of this woman expecting higher ideals and more perfect models for her identity. The old ones did not serve her anymore. Instead she identified with the thought that "The true sense of being and its eternal perfection should appear *now* . . . ."[107] And it did.

The healing work in Christian Science played a most important part in my life. Its introduction to me was, of course, quite a revolutionary idea because my own

106. *No.* 30:11
107. *S. & H.* 550:12-13 (Italics mine)

Protestant church was not awake then to the healing potential in its religious plan. But what we must understand is that healing is not the only revolutionary idea Christian Science gave to the world. More important than this is the Science of Celestial Being as I more clearly see it today, taught from Mrs. Eddy's highest consciousness and written in her textbook for all to understand and *for us* to courageously acknowledge. The progressive student does not let himself become involved spending time with erroneous claims. He knows that the "greater works" need his voice, his support and his promotion in a loving and sincere manner. They give him an opportunity to speak out from the premise of Oneness.

Let me repeat again: *"You* are the needed and the inevitable sponsors for the twentieth century, reaching deep down into the universal and rising above theorems into the transcendental, the infinite—yea, to the reality of God, man, nature, the universe."[108] Our work is to let the Science of Celestial Being *be revealed to us.* Thus we may prove that God-conscious identity as Principle is our continuing harmony of life. We are that very Principle *on this earth* and it is *here* that we demonstrate our knowledge and understanding of this eternal and spiritual fact.

No doubt you have noticed that I have been talking about several of the synonyms for God and, of course, Principle includes all of these. Now, however, I would like to share with you a few thoughts about the syn-

108. *My.* 248:14-18 (Italics mine).

onym: Mind. Every person here who has read *The Bridge* knows that the premise of it rests unreservedly on the statement that *All is Mind.* I bring this out repeatedly, and I explain this truth in many ways so that students realize of necessity that this Mind is their divine Mind. Again, it is not something belonging uniquely to God. The capitalization of the first letter M does not in truth declare this uniqueness. We do not consider that we have a lesser mind, called "mortal mind," with a little m as the first letter. We do not need to be working upward *toward* the divine Mind hoping to reach it sometime along the way in our progress. We accept the fact that the sense of all Godlike qualities is *our* divine consciousness now and always! The higher order of Science, our very own Mind, is our God-awareness, our Christ-thought, from which we are never separated, because we are never separated from Mind. This Mind manifests *us* and *we manifest it.*

In *Unity of Good,* page 24, line 2-4, we read, "I am the infinite All. From me proceedeth all Mind, all consciousness, all individuality, all being. My Mind is divine good . . ." This admission fills our consciousness completely with its omniscience. As we identify with it our revelation continues in a most divinely inspired and satisfying way. Admitting Mind as personal to us gives us present authority to investigate its infinite scope, to explore the depths of its richness. Self-existent, eternal, immortal, joyous and intelligent Mind! It is our very own spiritual integrity and maturity. It is our inventiveness, our endurance, our courage, elasticity and resiliance. It is *our Mind,* all-hearing, all-seeing, all-knowing, never outside of God's Oneness or Allness because we can't be outside of ourselves. As we stand

porter to the door of thought we move to the highest
meaning of Mind, understanding and appreciating its
divine location as the Kingdom of God within us. What
we feel and are expressing is the language which we
are. No doubt you have heard students of Christian
Science say many times that Mrs. Eddy had to state
Christian Science the way she did because if she had
been more outspoken it would not have been accepted
as a religion. Perhaps it would not have been so accepted in her time but this cannot be used as a valid
excuse today. The earnest and receptive student who
accepts the Mind of the Christ in the twentieth century is far more interested in the Science it advances.
We are living in this scientific age now, today, and this
is why we are more ready to identify as the Science of
Celestial Being. Not only inspiration and revelation but
reason and logic give us the glorious privilege of voic-
ing the more absolute statements with a conviction we
would not have had in Mrs. Eddy's time.

Undoubtedly this must have been a very revolu-
tionary statement for the apostle Paul to make in his
time: "Let this Mind be in *you,* which was also in
Christ Jesus." (Italics mine). Today we can accept it
as referring to ourselves, our person. This synonym for
God, Mind, is really ". . . The Only I, or Us; the only
Spirit, Soul, divine Principle, substance, Life, Truth,
Love . . ."[109] which we are.

Reading from *Misc. Writ.,* page 5:26-27, "That
man is the idea of infinite Mind, always perfect in
God, in Truth, Life, and Love, . . ." is great, but as
we go on reading the very next line we find this ". . . is

109. *S. & H.* 591:16-17

something not easily accepted . . ." because Mrs. Eddy feels this description of man is ". . . weighed down as is mortal thought with material beliefs." As students accepting the higher order of Science you have translated mortal thought and material beliefs into the state of blessings which they are; therefore you remain with the first portion of this quotation and identify *as* it, enjoying the perfect illustration of man: infinite Mind accepting its grand and glorious perfection!

In the question "What is Mind?" on page 469 of *S. & H.* (the chapter on *Recapitulation* where teachers are instructed which material to use for teaching a class) we find that Mind is not always ". . . the Only I or Us . . ." for we have to deal with another supposititious opposite of infinite Mind—called *devil* or evil [which] is not Mind . . ."

I am glad that Mrs. Eddy called it "supposititious" because the use of this word is an indication that sometimes she had doubts that evil existed at all. At other times it was very real to her and she counselled her members to protect themselves from it. In reference to this subject the use of the word means that evil is assumed to exist but is unsupported by fact. She gave this hypothetical opposite an identity, calling it "error," thus suggesting that in her reflection upon it she admitted its existence. As usual, if we go on reading this same paragraph about supposititious evil we find a return to the absolute thought where "evil can have no place, where all space is filled with God." As in so many instances *we have a choice* for our identification. Our authority is our divine Mind, and we keep it filled with Truth and Love for we need no other. There is just one Mind and we are it. We never will get closer to God-Mind than we do in the higher order of Identity.

Although this book is a record of 1973 class notes, I should like to add some thoughts that are appropriate here even though they relate to an event of 1974.

No Christian Scientist today would care to be identified with the satanism which is being shown in the film *The Exorcist,* a review of which I have read in *The National Observer,* January 26th, 1974, yet every student of orthodox Christian Science (and I was one of them) is instructed in the machinations of the devil, error, mortal mind, or, as often termed in Christian Science, "malicious animal magnetism." Not only must one study from the textbook the chapter on *Animal Magnetism Unmasked,* but also the repetitious Lesson-Sermon on *Ancient and Modern Necromancy, alias Mesmerism and Hypnotism, Denounced,* brought to him twice a year lest he forget! Someone offered me a copy of the *Third Edition* of *Science and Health* by Mary Baker Eddy. Believe it or not, I was crossing my bridge and I was unable to finish reading the forty-six pages of this edition which comprise the complete chapter entitled *Demonology.* And I know that the reason that I was unable to do so was that I was coming out of the dualism of Christian Science and approaching my higher order of Science.

On September 17, 1973, a Christian Science branch church gave all of its members certain citations for study under the heading *Admonition and Counsel.* Statements to be looked up were primarily to alert students to animal magnetism, mesmerism, the devil and error of all kind. One reference I shall quote is from *Misc. Writ.*, page 177:3-12: "The hour is come. The great battle of Armageddon is upon us. The powers of evil are leagued together in secret conspiracy against the Lord and against His Christ, as expressed and operative in Christian Science. Large numbers, in desperate malice, are engaged day and night in organizing action against us. Their feeling and purpose are deadly, and they have sworn enmity against the lives of our standard bearers." Interestingly, the next sentence is "What will you do about it?" I would like to tell every member of this dear church about the chapter in *The Bridge* entitled *The Translation of Animal Magnetism* where I have introduced the more rational acceptance of One Mind in place of the dualism of devil-versus-God, the mortal opposed to immortal Mind. I would ask them to identify with the One Mind only, and let these many citations dealing with this supposititious mind be beautifully translated to their true meaning.

As students in the higher order of Christian Science, our work in the instruction concerning dualism is ended. We need have no further concern with its presentation for the reason that we are identifying as God-consciousness in the Allness of Good which Mrs. Eddy also gave her students to work with as they advanced in the Science of Celestial Being.

You remember the story of the tares and the wheat, of course. Well, here is a new concept of them—no longer bad tares and the good wheat, but One!

CONSISTENCY IS PROGRESSION

I looked at my brother's field
And I saw tares
And I saw wheat.
But I wept over the tares
And forgot to joy
Over the wheat.

And then I thought
"I will try to rid him of his tares.
Yes, I will pull out these ugly weeds."
But instead now, I could see
Love was leading me
To see Its Presence as ALL
There is to everyone.
For Love is Life,
Is living me
Beholding Its manifestation
As ALL I see.[110]

The synonyms for God are not just word-terms such as Principle; Mind; Soul; Spirit; Life; Truth; Love. The definition of God points out emphatically that these synonyms are identified as God. They are interpreted this way throughout the textbook as well as in Mrs. Eddy's other works.

The whole purpose of this class, therefore, is to acquaint you with your own identity in such a way that you now understand that these terms defined as God are the terms you now define as yourself. In es-

---

110. Author Unknown

sence you identify as Principle; Mind; Soul; Spirit; Life; Truth; Love. This is your divine nature, the divine Science which you are. Probably the most important thing about identity or identification is that fundamentally it is a revelation! It is your God-conscious Identity revealing the Christ Science, a higher order of yourself. The moment you identify as this grand and inherent divinity something happens to you in such a way that you feel reborn, renewed, even though your divine nature was always present awaiting its *total* recognition. The meaning we take for "Identity" is sameness, Oneness, and the revelation of these grand definitions (synonyms) continues forever. I and my God are one.

So, as we approach Soul as one of the synonyms for God we recognize that this is a synonym relating to ourselves! You have done your work in the instruction of Christian Science and have studied the six synonyms for God, namely: Life, Truth, Love, Spirit, *Soul,* and Mind twice yearly. Now in the higher order of identification you accept its highest significance. Soul is the living, loving, pulsating exhilarating Sense which is felt so deeply and so richly within our being that we soar and sing and rejoice in the foreverness of it, our Soul-consciousness, God. The substance of Soul knows its ownness, feels it, lives it. Sure and satisfied with its infinite appearing as Mind in its infinite manifestation, Soul is appreciative, grateful for what it sees, hears and is aware of, heaven, here, present now. Soul is serene in knowing it *is!* And what and where it *is,* is what and where we are: God/Soul identity, here and now in our experience.

I invite you to identify also with the definition of this

synonym given to us in *Webster's Collegiate Dictionary*:
"The seat of real life, vitality, or action; animating or
vital principle . . . Courage; spirit; fervor; spiritual
force." What a great synonym Soul is! In the knowledge that this Soul-consciousness is your own God-consciousness (one and the same thing) you have no further need to separate *soul* from *Soul*. Are you ready to
identify as this: "I, or EGO. Divine Principle; Spirit;
Soul . . ,"[111] and this: "The divine Mind is the Soul
of man, and gives man dominion over all things . . .
his province is in spiritual statutes, in the higher law
of Mind"?[112] Isn't this something wonderful for our
identification: "Man is the expression of Soul"![113] Note
here: it is not a *reflection* of Soul, but the *expression!*

There may be no synonym for God that requires so
much translation as the one for Soul. The student
(through the instruction) has more metaphysical work
identifying with this synonym than with any other because he has to free himself from the dualism which
seems to be very evident. Mrs. Eddy may not have had
an easy time putting her ideas across on this subject,
for we find that in one quarter the Lesson-Sermon subject is *Soul,* which is considered as a synonym for God.
In the next quarter the Lesson-Sermon considers the
subject: *Soul and Body.* In studying these different
Lesson-Sermons, the student soon recognizes that the
lesson on *Soul* represents a higher order of Science. In
Soul and Body the student finds a more dualistic approach to Soul because his work must usually compare
Soul as immortal with Body as mortal. However, *we*

111. *S. & H.* 588:9 (to;)
112. *S. & H.* 307:25-26, 29-30
113. *S. & H.* 477:26

do not wrestle with Soul versus Body. We have reached that place where we know they are One! The God-conscious Soul/Body is the infinite appearing of the allness which we are and, I must add, *here in the flesh.*

I was explaining this higher order of Soul to a person one day and she said, "But you know the poem, 'Only God can make a tree'." I simply reminded her that if she were not here as body, as Soul, as God-conscious Mind, there would be no tree for her to experience at all. It is the presence of herself, her identity as individual knowledge, that is the essential spiritual substance of her being which sees, and feels and smells the tree. "... Soul is never without its representative."[114] Then the presence of her Self permits the presence of the tree! And I invited her happily back to the words: "I was the world I wandered through" in the poem, *Morning In Spring,* on page 343 of *The Bridge.* Let us not sell ourselves short anymore. "... (in absolute Science) Soul, or God, is the only truth-giver to man.[115] How very important is your identification as Soul! You are the nature-loving Soul/Sense that feels and enjoys your physicality because you have translated it and you appreciate its glory.

Soul is kind, gracious, understanding and always prepared to *be* Love; it is the forgiver and the forgetter. Soul is the human being which is the divine and the divine being which is human. Soul encompasses all that the eye and ear perceive because it reaches the depth of Being and finds repose in Mind's infinite see-

---

114. *S. & H.* 427:4-5
115. *S. & H.* 72:11-12

ing and hearing. Soul is the enthusiastic Spirit of *your* being; it is where you are, and where you are God is.

I want to spend the rest of the time with the synonym for God which is Love. I feel very strongly that it is most important in the healing part of Christian Science, and, like the other synonyms for God, for yourself, it is all-inclusive. In our living Principle, Mind, Soul, Spirit, Life, and Truth consciously as personal identity, we are Love. For Love to be love, it needs to be felt by us inwardly as a demonstrated impression of itself, indelibly stamped within our consciousness. Love not only lives to love, but it loves to live. Perhaps this is a good place to let you know that whether you read the word love with a small l or the word with a capital L, from the idea of Identity which we are accepting *l*ove and *L*ove mean the same thing—and this goes for all the other synonyms as well. The moment you find yourself making a distinction you have consciously created a separateness.

As students within the instruction we were continually confronted with the Life divine and the life human, the Truth and the truth, mortal mind and Mind immortal! Using our present understanding we have the grand opportunity to build a bridge to connect these, to integrate them, to see their likenesses, their correspondence.

In *My.* 185:16-17 we read "Life is the spontaneity of Love, inseparable from Love . . ." and we identify with this thought. We let love enter every phase of our living; its presence is made known to us by the harmony and peace we have. This is how we know it is with us. Love is the one synonym we questioned very often in orthodox Christian Science because we were not always sure how it was to be demonstrated. We had mixed feelings about its meaning. When we decided what it meant in a given situation we were not always sure that we were expressing the right degree; the differences between the personal and the impersonal concepts of Love could be very frustrating. Sometimes it seemed we gave enough, sometimes too much. I saw this happen very recently. Two women visited me in my home. I noticed that one of them had difficulty in walking; apparently she was not easily able to see the floor. They were both Christian Scientists. I found myself guiding her, taking her hand, showing a loving, personal concern. I had the feeling that my other friend was trying to be impersonal by ignoring the difficulty, presumably holding metaphysically to her friend's perfection. I, too, thought this way about her, but, as stated in *The Bridge,* we do the human thing, the compassionate, loving thing, because we know now that human activity and love are divine activity and Love.

Our love as expression does not deny us the ability to maintain our friend's perfection. But we do not ignore the human concept; it is the divine concept: *Man, Present Being.* Person is not and can never be separated from the infinite Love which he is. We are no longer the impersonal priest who saw the wounded man and "passed by on the other side," but rather the certain Samaritan, who, when he saw the wounded man, ". . . came where he was; and when he saw him, he had compassion on him . . . bound up his wounds, pouring oil and wine, . . . and took care of him."

(*Luke* 10:30-34). In the higher order of Love we take care of the divine person, Man, physically/metaphysically.

Although traditionally we are taught about the impersonal side of Love, this has conflicted many times with the warmth and affection of personal love. In the higher order of Christian Science we have a new identity for this synonym, and it reaches far beyond what we have been taught in the instruction. With our new view we can express personal tenderness and loving compassion as part of the entire Love spectrum!

The religiousness of our church often made us too easily content with the statement that God is Love. It was enough to rest on this, but the effect in many instances was to preoccupy us with loving God to the extent that we neglected to love the very ones who were near and dear to us. Should we not love *them* as much as we would worship God? Loving them *is* worshipping God, for in this we are identifying them with their divinity and ourselves with a higher order of Love.

We might paraphrase the song I mentioned previously in this manner: "Let there be love on earth, and let it begin with me." Every year that I hear the Christmas Carol "Oh, come let us adore Him, O come let us adore Him, Christ, the Lord," I feel as all do who have been brought up to see it as part of the story of Jesus' birth. I like to think, however, and with no irreverence, of course, that if Jesus did return to us on earth he would tell us all to stop adoring him and to get on with the business of adoring each other. *The Bridge* shows the great respect I have for Jesus, the *person,* the *man,* the *Christ,* and what I have shared with you today supports this. But as we look into what the word "adore" means, aside from its meaning of reverence, we find it also is an expression which honors divinity.

At a dinner one night in the home of some friends my husband and I were pleasantly surprised to find the host and hostess suggesting we hold hands with those sitting on either side of us as part of an expression of grace. They said it meant a reverence for each other. Grace was not something related only to gratitude for food but it was also for each other's presence. I was deeply touched by the warmth of love that we felt. This is some of what I have been talking about in this seminar, not only identifying with the holiness which is ours but with that which is all others' as well. We have great regard for the dignity and the divinity of each I AM that is present here today, and we extend this to everyone in our universe. Let us magnify it, this love that is another attribute of God. Jesus gave us a new commandment: that we should *love one another*. By this he meant that we should respect and honor each other as prayerfully as we honor our own God-concept.

Communication is most important here because it leads us to the heart and soul of Love. I do not mean only verbal communication, for on some occasions it is the unsaid word that is needed for peace and contentment. There are, of course, many other ways than verbal ones for us to use and as we develop these ways our Love is divinely directed for its expression in them.

Some time ago a woman called me to talk about her family. She was very unhappy about her situation, and to help me understand all that was happening she suggested that I come to her home and have dinner with them. It was an unusual request. I certainly could have given her some pertinent and truthful statements over the phone, but the earnestness in her voice and the urgency of her invitation made me feel that I should accept it.

Soon after I arrived we sat down at the dinner table. There we were: mother, father, two sons, a daughter and myself. As a kind of statement of grace the daughter repeated the Scientific Statement of Being before the meal began, but she spoke as though she felt she had to hurry up and get it over with. My own thoughts at the moment were that if we really paid any attention to the words we might not have the meal at all, for the first statement is "There is no life, truth, intelligence nor substance in matter . . ."—that is, from the orthodox point of view! However, the meal was satisfying to all I am sure, but for a long time there was not a single word of communication. When one of the sons finally spoke, it was with an expression of hostility and criticism of his mother. The father said nothing at all, then or after dinner. Toward me they showed a simple and quiet respect. I kept my joy, knowing that I was sitting in the presence of Love itself.

The needed healing in that family did not happen overnight. Subsequently, however, I was able to watch a beautiful transformation take place as the mother grew to where she did not expect everyone to be like herself, to think exactly as she did, and to do everything the way she thought it should be done. Gradually she saw them as individuals, unique and divinely so. As she came to understand a fuller meaning of Love, her domination, her self-will and critical judgment of them, turned to one of respect and tenderness. Soon she received these qualities back from them. In other words, she lived her love differently and in her living this new way the whole atmosphere in her home changed. Her concept had reached a higher order.

The present generation, sometimes referred to as "The Love Generation," is wonderfully awake to this synonym. We see the word "Love" on stamps and stickers on their car bumpers, and while we may not always be in full accord with their methods and their associations, this new generation's concept of Love is upon us, insisting that we acknowledge its presentation and the mood in which it is appearing. We may reject it or we may accept it, in our affirmation that "All is infinite Mind . . ." for *choice* is one of the conditions we include with this statement.

As I now see it, traditional Christian Science appears to have been responsible for our adopting an impersonal type of love for both God and man. The "thou-shalt-nots" certainly filled us with guilt about our natural feelings, so much so that we came to regard them as evil. I don't mind telling you right here that when I received my first kiss from a young man, I was stating, mentally, of course, that there was no sensation in matter!

Certainly in our orthodoxy it was difficult for us to appreciate the warmth of personal affection. Love for God was always kept on the top of the list; love for person was another thing. Of course I am aware that I am talking about just a small part of the greatest thing in the world. Love is so infinite that talking and writing about it merely touches the surface of its greatness. But surely, part of this wonderful synonym which we are is the feeling we consistently hold to and express in our lives moment by moment. More than this, for love to be love it must reach out and beyond our personal world to be Love's Allness. We find, then, that it takes on *infinite* proportions in our lives where we are at the moment. The opportunities to express our understanding of it are many *as we identify as Love.*

When my sister's husband passed on she was filled with grief. Her self-pity and the sense of loss she experienced were so great she had no love to give to her children, also saddened at the loss of their father. She felt her situation so deeply that for a time she believed herself separated from divine Love. My sister is a Christian Scientist. I took her aside and explained that she now had a very important work to do. She needed to identify as Love itself in this situation. She listened when I told her she was needed *to be the Christ,* the Comforter, to her family, and I meant that she should be warm, loving and compassionate as a *personal mother.* Her receptivity was immediate; her Father-Mother God shone through beautifully. I watched the power of Love heal not only herself but those about her. I saw an atmosphere of grief and loss change into one of activated love and an awareness of eternal life.

We know that Christian Scientists avoid funerals if they possibly can because they do not want to make a reality of death. However, in accepting the unreality of this event they are not in a position to be the Comforter to the living, who need the spiritual love and scientific understanding that life is eternal. Our presence on such an occasion declares this great truth to be all-in-all!

I have a friend who told me that while she was a member of the Christian Science organization she never inquired of anyone "How are *you* today?" because inquiries of this sort were not considered appropriate. I reminded her that in the higher order of Love warmth and tenderness are integral parts of this synonym as she identifies with it, and that it is divinely natural for her not only to express feelings of brotherliness, interest and affection for others, but to expect them for herself.

Sometimes a single act of love has tremendous significance. Has it ever occurred to you that when Jesus said to his disciples, ". . . Follow me and let the dead bury their dead,"[116] the entire story which we now have might be very different if they had all obeyed his command *literally* on every occasion? In this case, fortunately, there was ". . . a rich man of Arimathaea, named Joseph, who also himself was Jesus' disciple."[117] and after the crucifixion he thought that perhaps he was not supposed to hold to the letter of his master's saying necessarily. He asked for Jesus' body and placed it in his own tomb. It was *his* way of identifying with the synonym, Love. This act made remarkably possible the continuing historical account of Jesus' life— his three days in the sepulchre and his resurrection, in turn followed by that grand and glorious culmination which we call the ascension.

Love is understanding all situations and conditions; Love forgives and forgets; Love attains its highest level by being the love which Love is.

---

116. *Matthew*: 8:22
117. *Matthew*: 27:57

In concluding today's seminar may I read this poem while you identify as it!

INTERLUDE

LXVIII.

BEHOLD, this is a new day! ...
  The Past is ended!
  Come now
And let thine eyes be Truth and Love;
  And to-day
Abide in the Present, and realize God's Presence!
Lo! all is good and beautiful to-day!
Thy being is encompassed in the Great Reality!
From the centre of all the sun of life and power
  Radiates everywhere:
And from the centre of thy life, the divine Consciousness, sun of thy being, radiates now with healing power unto thy every part and thy every circumstance!
Then wilt thou realize more and more the freedom and the beauty, the love and the truth, of thy real nature.
Through all there breathes a divine interior warmth, the Holy Breath.
The Love of God, all pervading, works as a silent energy, transforming, renewing, recreating all things after the perfect pattern, God's thought,
  Unto a perfect and beautiful expression!
  Within thy nature is the Holy substance,
  Within thy consciousness the Divine Wisdom,
Showing through thy way and form radiant love and beauty.
  In perfect humility

On the bed-rock of thy being thou standest, . . .
    And lo! the Light shines, and becomes manifest
      in thee!
The eternal is the Present, and thou dost
Dwell therein in the sincerity of the clear vision,
    Open to the Presence,
Expressing the beautiful Word of Truth,
And Love is with thee wheresoever thou goest![118]

———————

118. Richard Whitwell: *The Cloud and the Fire*. H. T. Hamblin, Bosham, Chichester, England, pages 57 and 58, N.D.

POEMS

127

BIBLIOGRAPHY

Adair, James, and Ted Miller. *We Found Our Way Out*. Baker Book House, Grand Rapids, Michigan. 1964.

Bach, Richard, *Jonathan Livingston Seagull*. The Macmillan Co., New York. 1970.

Braden, Charles S. *Spirits in Rebellion*. Southern Methodist University Press, Dallas, Texas. 1963.

Christian Science Hymnal. The Christian Science Publishing Society, Boston, Massachusetts. 1932.

Clark, Glenn. *The Man Who Tapped The Secrets Of The Universe*. Macalester Park Publishers, 1969.

Eddy, Mary Baker. *Science and Health with Key to the Scriptures*. Published by the Trustees under the Will of Mary Baker G. Eddy, Boston, Massachusetts. 1910.

—— *Prose Works other than Science and Health*, Published by The Trustees under the Will of Mary Baker G. Eddy, Boston. 1925.

Gibran, Kahlil. *The Prophet*. Random House, New York, 1951.

Laird, Margaret, C.S.B. *The Laird Letter*. The Margaret Laird Foundation. 10578 Le Conte Avenue, Los Angeles, California. January/February 1972. Vol. 19, No. 1.

Longfellow, Henry Wadsworth. *The Complete Poetical Works of Longfellow*. Houghton Mifflin Co., Boston, Massachusetts. 1922.

Merritt, Robert, and Arthur Corey. *Christian Science & Liberty*. DeVorss & Co., Santa Monica, California. 1970.

Moore, Irene, C.S. *The Bridge*. DeVorss & Co., Santa Monica, California. 1971.

Oxford Book of English Mystical Verse, The. Oxford, At the Clarendon Press. 1953.

129

Pope, Alexander. *Selected Works*. Modern Library. New York. 1948.

Smith, Cushing, C.S.B. *I Can Heal Myself And I Will*. Frederick Fell, Inc., New York. 1962.

Spalding, Baird T. *Life and Teaching of The Masters of The Far East*, Volume IV. DeVorss & Co., Santa Monica, California. 1948.

Teale, Edwin Way. *The Wilderness World of John Muir*. Houghton Mifflin Co., Boston, Massachusetts. 1954.

Toffler, Alvin. *Future Shock*. Random House, New York. 1970.

Tolstoy, Leo. *War and Peace*. Random House, New York. N.D.

Troward, Thomas. *The Edinburgh Lectures on Mental Science*. Dodd, Mead & Company, New York. 1909.

Whitwell, Richard. *The Cloud and the Fire*. H. T. Hamblin, Publisher, Bosham, Chichester, England. N.D.